Healing the Warrior Heart

A Glimpse into the Hearts of Combat Veterans and their Supporting Loved Ones

---

Andrew R. Jones
USMC Combat Veteran

Copyright © 2013 by Andrew R. Jones. All rights reserved.
ISBN 978-1492193012

Healing Warrior Heart published by **Triumph Press**
www.TriumphPress.com

Cover Artwork: Mariah Hudson
Layout and design: ipublicidades.com

10 9 8 7 6 5 4 3 2 1

This book is brought to you by:

Love Your Veterans is a national campaign to
raise awareness, appreciation and support for our
military heroes. This is done through the discovery
and sharing of their *Triumph Stories* which brings
healing purpose and meaning to our protectors
while preserving the important stories of our
nation's legacy; putting a face, name and life to the
word veteran. It is only by knowing our heroes,
their wisdom and stories, that we love our veterans
enough to care for them the way they deserve and
need!

To learn how you can support the preservation
of our nation's hero legacies,

Go to ***www.LoveYourVeterans.org***

Acknowledgments

To God
Thank You for being a forgiving God and for walking beside me
after I cursed You for neglect. My faith is with You and my heart
is open to Your guidance.

To Crazy Monkey and Dump Truck
Your purity and innocence warms my heart with every smile and laugh.
Hearing, "I love you Daddy," is all I need to keep pushing
forward to the next day.

To Chelsea, my Angel
Your everlasting support and love pulled me out of a dark cave when
I thought I was lost forever. Your patience, tolerance and stubbornness
are truly gifts from God. I love you with all my heart and
look forward to the rest of our lives together.

To my family
Mom, Dad, Laurie, Kenny, Kim, Bet, James
R.I.P. Grandma, Grandpa and Rich
We have our moments of insanity and lack of judgment. We have been
stretched apart and brought back together more times than a rubber band.
But how boring of a family would we be if wasn't the case?
I cherish each and every one of you.

To Julie, Ryry and Chloe
You accepted me into your life and somehow found the patience
and tolerance to support me along my journey of healing.
Although all three of you have caused me some level of craziness,
I love you with all my heart.

To my PTSD Counselor Danny Guckenburg
God bless you and your patience.
My life would not be the same without you.

To my Life Coach Betty Merritt
I never knew what true hope and healing was until you touched me.
An unexplainable energy flows through your hands and
no doubt exists in my mind, The Universe guided me to you.

To the Marines of Fox Company 2nd Bn 23rd Marines,
Sinners & Saints Regimental Combat Team 1,
Operation Iraqi Freedom, Spring Break 2003

The greatest group of fighting men ever to walk The Valley of the
Shadow of Death. We tore through the enemy like rabid dogs and
displayed compassion to those in need. We epitomized
the title of United States Marines.

To all who have been a part of my life, I am thankful for our experiences
together. Each of you are a significant part of how I arrived to this part
of my journey. Thank you for seeing me through my darkest hours.

Organization Acknowledgements

An enormous amount of my gratitude goes to Melanie Davis, Founder *of Love Your Veterans*, and Military Author Kevin E. Lake for putting me in contact with her. Without Love Your Veterans, this book would not be possible and would never reach full potential. Thank you for your guidance and support in this journey of healing. I look forward to many years of excellence in our missions together.

www.loveyourveterans.org
www.facebook.com/LoveYourVeterans
Info@LoveYourVeterans.org

To Patricia Clason, Founder of Healing Warrior Hearts. Your contributions to my mission of healing and reaching out to others is received with arms of deep gratitude. I pray for your continued success in helping Veterans reach a sense of peace.

www.starfishfound.org/veterans/
www.facebook.com/HealingWarriorHearts
warriorheart@starfishfound.org
(414) 374-5433
Milwaukee, WI

To Richard Brewer, Founder of One Warrior Won. Thank you for your support and motivation throughout the creation of this book. Through your voice and your mission with One Warrior Won, you will continue to make a difference for Veterans. Much love, God bless and Semper Fi.

www.onewarriorwon.org
www.facebook.com/onewarriorwon
Rich@onewarriorwon.org
(207) 632-0893
Portland, ME

To Betty Merritt and the entire staff of The Merritt Center of Arizona.
Attending your Bootcamp for Life program for Combat Veterans
changed my life. I was in a dark place and desperate to find light.
I not only found it; it consumed me and made me a different man.
A man with a future, not afraid to accept true joy into my heart.
You are a miracle worker.
www.merrittcenter.org
betty@merrittcenter.org
(928) 474-4268
Payson, AZ

The Manawale'a Riding Center in Hawaii provides Equestrian Therapy
for veterans and is a wonderful Non-Profit Organization ran by people
with pure hearts wanting to help. Many organizations such as this exist
in all parts of the country and deserve much needed attention. Please
contact them and show your support.
www.manawalea.org
manawalea2000@yahoo.com
(808) 352-1523
Waimanalo, HI 96795

Praise for Healing Warrior Heart

"Adversity deepens the soul and expands wisdom. The horror of war is the hottest fire of adversity to endure. Those who come out on the other side of these flames, and write about it, bring to the world the most treasured words of all… the refining from such heat makes them exceptional. Andrew Jones is a combat veteran whose thoughts and words strike deep in the hearts of his comrades-in-arms, bringing profound healing. In "Healing Warrior Heart," Andrew combines his works with those of many other veterans and their supporting loved ones into a powerful and profound anthology which will heal all who read it; veteran or civilian."

-Melanie Davis, Founder of *Love Your Veterans*

"Andrew takes the written word and turns it into an emotion filled journey. While working on his own healing, he opens the mind and takes along passengers to the foreground of PTSD. He is definitely one of the most talented Military Authors of our time."

-Karen Barker, Author *I Never Saw It Coming*

"Andrew's writings paint a vivid picture of the costs of war, giving a voice to many who have endured death, sorrow and the guilt of losing friends. He also shows there is still hope, love and the Almighty to bring the suffering back into the light of peace. Andrew Jones has touched my heart and the depth of my soul with his poems and stories. He has stepped up as a leader, gathering others to write about their experiences as he struggles to find his way out of the dark and painful hole of PTSD. I strongly believe we will see more from Andrew Jones in the future."

-Alberta J. Lindley, U.S. Army Veteran '79-'92

"I have read several of Andrew R. Jones' poems. To say the man has talent is an understatement. His prose goes directly to the heart and the jugular. Some will hit hard and some will sneak up on you. If you want to know what a survivor is, read these poems, put them down and then come back to them. These poems are hard-hitting and gritty, but shows an inner tenderness that is rare. I look forward to reading more."

-Karen Salamone-Jourdan, Author of *Gabriel's Gate*

"Andrew R. Jones is a godsend. His writings really hit home… I see now I have the scars inside and out but because of being sick I have always been ashamed of serving. I have always looked at it as a mistake that messed up my mind. In time I hope I can have the heart he has."

-Jason Schooley, U.S. Army Veteran '96-'00

"A man with so many experiences, who participated in perhaps the bloodiest, most active part of any war in modern history, has many ghosts behind his eyes. Sleep doesn't always come easy, and inner peace is a luxury he wishes he could afford on a regular basis; but to come home and 'get over it,' or be able to 'leave the past in the past' is a struggle for Jones as much as any other combat veteran. Fortunately, he has his writing. And he's damn good at it! But don't take my word for it. The proof is in the pudding."

-Kevin E. Lake, Author of *Off Switch*

"It's been many years since I have seen Corporal Andrew Jones. I remember a young, quiet Marine, one whom I honored to have served with during the beginning of the War on Terror.

Corporal Jones, like all Marine Non Commissioned Officers served not for himself, but for his Marines. He lived his life as a Leader of Marines, day in and day out for the Marines to his left and right. Corporal Jones and so many other Combat Veterans never really come home, their lives forever changed by the reality of war. What he experienced, cannot be fully understood by anyone who has never shouldered a weapon. To kill and to survive, is to die from within.

Many of his fellow Fox Company Veterans still carry a heavy pack, one full of guilt, anger, hatred, remorse, and frustration. It is a pack they want so much to drop and walk away from. To rid themselves of a pack that has been digging into their shoulders and shattered souls is not an easy task. Each Marine digs in, fighting to free himself from the memories that have become nightmares. Some Marines turn to family for support. Others turn to their God to find peace. There are some that have neither God nor Family and they find temporary comfort in drugs and alcohol. For Corporal Andrew Jones, it was the gift of writing that has enabled him to express his feelings. He has put down on paper his inner thoughts, harnessing his anger, and frustrations. His words are powerful, moving and meaningful. Poems that enable the Warriors reading them to put into perspective their own experiences and find peace knowing they are not alone.

This book inspired me to look deep within myself and find the strength to ground my own pack. Through his words I have begun to find the peace that I have been searching for since I retired from the Corps.

Corporal Jones continues to lead his fellow Marines in their fight to find peace with the gift God has given him as a writer. His selfless devotion to his brothers is how I will remember him. A quiet Marine with a heart of gold."

-Sergeant Major Nick Anthony Lopez USMC (Ret)

TABLE OF CONTENTS

Foreword Poem

You
Chelsea Labarr
Dedicated to Andrew R. Jones

I feel okay by myself
I prefer to be alone
Nothing will hurt this heart of mine
Lined with ice and stone

You show up with that smile, those beautiful eyes
I cover with a blanket of fear
The things you say, the way you feel
Is it real? Are you being sincere?

What's happening to me? I'm being so dumb
Craving your opinion, and touch
This is my stop. I can travel no more
God, I just want you so much

I need it to end; this is going too far
Driving, keeping tears at bay
Open my mouth, but hear your words
And decide to hear what you say

The best decision I've ever made
The only one able to touch
My heart through all the cold and stone
Andrew, I love you so much.

No fear of who you are
I know your heart is true
This story wouldn't have worked
If it had been anyone else but you.

Prayer from the Author

Dear Lord, I thank You for never leaving my side, even during the times I was convinced You forgot me. Thank You for being a forgiving God and a loving Father. Thank You for having enough love for me to allow me to fall and to walk the dark alley of despair. For I truly believe, without having felt true pain, one will never understand the worth of true joy. Thank You for showing me Your awesomeness the day I fell to my knees. For even after cursing You, my heart opened and received Your love and Your voice. My faith is strong and I have turned my control over to Your care. May You find the words in this book worthy of praise and may You distribute these words to all of the men and women in need of healing.

In the Lord's Name I pray, Amen.

Note to the Reader

This book is a dream, miraculously transformed into a reality. When I began writing, I did it for the sole purpose of my own healing; sharing with only those closest to me and hesitant to do so. I debated on sharing with the Marines from my unit, in fear it may trigger memories they found a way to deal with. I felt it selfish to share my thoughts and problems with brothers who seemed to be doing fine. Throughout the years, I struggled with my demons of war, bringing about: two divorces, months in county jail, countless street fights, substance abuse, losing custody of my children, unstable employment, an uncontrollable rage causing me to lay hands on my sister, frighten my mother to tears and scream in my father's face. Worst of all was the time my oldest son, 4 years old at the time, stood between me and his mother and pleaded, "Daddy, stop yelling!" I dreaded the possibility of releasing those demons onto my brothers. Undoubtedly, the writing helped me and I became convinced it could only help others. So I shared a story about a battle we had in Al Gharraf, Iraq. It was received with positive feedback and comments about how they also remember and think about it daily. From that moment, I had to continue writing and sharing my words with others who may also be in pain. My stories and poems were sent to literary journals and magazines and published with excitement. The more I wrote and the more I shared; the more eyes I opened and the more hearts I inspired to begin healing.

When beginning the process of putting **Healing Warrior Heart** together, I intended to only use my poems and short stories. Then the idea came to include a few other veterans who may have done some writing. I put out the word for submissions of poems and short stories and was quickly overwhelmed with veterans and family members emailing their work. Some were previously published, some dug out old journals and crumbled sheets of paper from years past and some emailed saying, "I don't even know why I'm sending you this." The desire for veterans and their family members to be heard is an envious one. We have a voice and it happens to be powerful, filled with passion and inspiration.

My mission, is to provide an outlet for all veterans and their supporting loved ones to open their hearts and shout to the world, "I'm still here! Don't forget about me!" The poems and stories which lie ahead will invoke emotions of all ranges and may bring to life emotions you thought were dead. The most difficult part of the road to healing is making the decision to start the journey. Weakness is not a label carried by occupants of this road. Strength and dedication surround us and we must keep our eyes open to see we are not alone. The only place loneliness and fear are able to prosper is in the dark cave of solitude too many veterans and their family members crawl into. If you are in that cave, I challenge you to crawl outside with squinted eyes, stand on two feet with aching bones and reach out a hand for another brother or sister to grab on to.

Healing Warrior Heart is only the beginning of many more projects to come in the near future. Through networking with veteran's organizations and individuals seeking to help, I am determined to make a difference in the way society views and treats its veterans and their families. Join me in this mission and let our voices be heard. Enjoy your journey through the pages awaiting you. Much love and God bless.

-Andrew R. Jones
Corporal, 0351
USMC '99-'06

"Only the dead have seen the end of war."
-Plato

Al Gharraf
Andrew R Jones

*Marines of Fox Co 2/23 charging to a position of cover during
the Battle of Al Gharraf, Iraq March 2003*

It was dark.

No. It was beyond dark.

It was beyond any darkness I had ever experienced.

It was the complete and absolute absence of light.

Night Vision Goggles (NVG's) were useless because they needed the slightest bit of light to operate. "Getting used to it" or waiting for your eyes to dilate was not an option. There was nothing to see. The world was completely void of light and overtaken by darkness. The day was Tuesday, March 25, 2003, in Al Gharraf, Iraq.

Earlier, our company pushed through An Nasiryah, taking small arms fire and encountering our first sight of death. Bodies littered the streets, torn to pieces, flattened to the asphalt by tanks and trucks. Their blood spilled out beside them.

After fighting our way through this city, recently plagued with death and destruction, we received a distress call. Alpha Battery 1/11 had been ambushed north of our position and had casualties. They needed help, and they needed it fast. Excitement rushed over me as the trucks accelerated and we received orders. Five days into the war and we were finally going to see some real action. This is what war stories were made of and I was about to make mine. What a stupid little shit I was. The convoy pulled off the road as we started taking fire. Bullets ricocheted as we dismounted the trucks and a feeling of calm swept over me. I wanted to get in the action and do my part.

I wanted to kill.

Roxley and I dismounted and rushed to the road side where our brothers were laying down heavy fire into the town across the street.

I reached the position, but something was wrong. Where was Roxley? He was right behind me. I looked back and saw a sight that will haunt me for eternity. Now I'll admit, it could've been worse. He wasn't dead, nor did he die, and until my dying day I will testify he is alive due to the grace of God, not the inaccurate shooting of the enemy. He always had a force field around him and when he was near me, it extended around me as well. He was a man of God and he had the strongest faith I had ever seen.

There was Roxley, low crawling in the dirt about 20 meters back. Struggling, exerting all bits of energy and looking helpless as he tried to make it to the road side. Bullet after bullet ricocheted around his body and flew over his head.

Did I go get him? Did I rush back and grab him and help him get to the road side to a safer position of cover? No. I stared at him and his situation and all I could do was yell.

"Let's go Rox, HURRY UP!"

Yea, because yelling at him was going to save his life. Yelling at him was going to protect his body from the one bullet that found him. Like I said, what a stupid little shit I was. Roxley made it to the roadside and to this day holds no hard feelings for my inaction. But seeing him in that situation replays in my head every day and haunts my dreams at night;

because, in my dreams, he doesn't survive. His force field fails him and he dies 5 meters from my arms with a gunshot to the face.

Why does that happen in my dreams? Because in reality, that is what should've happened.

I was too weak to rush to him.

I was too weak to protect him.

Roxley made it to the roadside and we loaded the SMAW. We acquired a target about 150 meters across the street and aimed in to blow it to hell. *CRACK!!!* A bullet struck the asphalt, shooting rocks into my face. I looked at Roxley as I felt for blood and he gave me the thumbs up.

"You're ok; you're ok!"

There he is comforting me, just seconds after I left him in the dirt.

I'm ok.

Rox told me I'm ok so it must be true. I aimed in again and sent 83mm of destruction down range. *BOOM!* The fiery explosion destroyed the building. What made that my target? The bastard running into it as he was holding a baby in one arm and shooting an AK-47 with the other; as well as the barrage of gun fire coming from multiple windows. That was over; time to acquire the next target. *BOOM!!!* Another rocket down range, another fiery explosion in another building filled with these bastards, children, mothers and God knows who else. The battle shifted and we dropped back to a support position as tanks and tracks rolled in. They sent their own barrage of fire into the town; leveling buildings and homes.

The unit started regrouping to mount trucks and move out. But then it came. What the Iraqis refer to as *Shamal,* The Mother of All Sandstorms. A sandstorm of biblical proportions. A sandstorm that only hit this hard on very rare occasions. This was *The Nothing.* It engulfed everything around us. It ate the light from the world. Instead of moving out, orders came down to stay put and hold our position until morning. There was no air support available and all units were to standby in their location. It's not like we could've gone anywhere if we tried. There was nowhere to go. There was nothing. The sun descended and the world went from dark brown to black. A blink of the eye went unnoticed. This is where it began.

My night in Hell.

Roxley and I held our position and stayed close, never losing touch of the other. Every voice seemed distant, no matter how close the Marine was. I felt alone. We decided to try and sleep. Maybe it would all be better when I woke up. Maybe the world would be visible again. But how could one sleep? Only a couple hundred meters across the street was the village we helped destroy; a village dealing with death and destruction. They did not go quietly into the night. They did not pick up their dead and go to sleep.

No.

They screamed.

They screamed in terror. Mothers screamed as they were undoubtedly holding their children. Children screamed as they were undoubtedly holding their mothers.

That smell. What was that smell? Sewage? Trash? No. It came over me without a sprinkle of doubt.

Death.

Flesh being burned. Fires cracked from the village as bodies burned. Screams filled the distant air as mothers and children grieved their loss we so proudly handed them.

We were in Hell.

A sandstorm didn't block out the sky. We fell into the pits of Hell.

Darkness, screams, death.

Isn't that what Hell is? This night has to eventually end right? Time must continue moving no matter what the weather is like or no matter the situation, right? Wait it out. Go to sleep. Plug my ears. Pull my flak jacket over my face to mask the smell. It's not real. It's just my imagination. This doesn't happen in real life. This isn't real. It's just a dream. Wake up! WAKE THE FUCK UP!

No. It was real. The news articles say it was real. The First Sergeant from Alpha Battery 1/11 who later thanked us for their rescue said it was real. Every night of my life I have found courage to lie in bed and close my eyes has proved it was real. Every scream from a woman or child has told me it was real. But every night it's just a nightmare; sick and twisted nightmare that on occasion I can scream my way out of. Maybe it never actually happened. Maybe it has just been a nightmare all along. Maybe I'm just crazy. No. It was real.

Morning came, dust began to clear and we moved out to the next mission; leaving Al Gharraf and Tuesday March 25, 2003 physically behind us. But never mentally. Mentally, I will never leave. I will be stuck in this night in Hell. One day it will be over. One day I will rest. One day I will find peace.

One day.

The Warrior Heart
Andrew R. Jones

*Corporal Andrew R. Jones petting a stray Iraqi dog
which befriended him for several days*

Gaze into a Warrior's eyes
Through the guilt
Through the shame
The 1,000 yard stare of pain
Exists a level of passion
Never to be tamed

The Warrior Heart is passionate
Full of love and grace
Praise be to those
Willing to stand and face

Gaze into a Warrior's soul
Through the darkness
Through the storm
The fallen brothers he mourns
Exists a level of passion
Never to be torn

The Warrior Heart is passionate
Full of love and grace
Praise be to those
Seeing beyond a stone face

Breathe in the Warrior's scent
Through the whiskey
Through the beer
Gallons upon gallons of tears
Exists a level of passion
Never to be feared

The Warrior Heart is passionate
Full of love and grace
Unfortunate are those
Who have never felt its embrace

"Be strong and courageous. Do not be terrified, do not be discouraged, for the Lord your God will be with you wherever you go."
-Joshua 1:9

My Testimony
Andrew R. Jones

Are You so magnificent?
That I can be so insignificant?

Will You know who I am?
When I stand to be judged?
What will You remember?

Dancing in the rain? Or
Drinking away the pain?
Love in my heart? Or
Hate in my eyes?

Will You know who I am?
When I stand to be judged?
What will You remember?

We made a deal in Baghdad
Do You remember?
When You shielded me from impact
"Ok I believe!" I said
"Get me home and we'll talk."
But I failed to predict Your neglect

When I envisioned a knife
Entering my wife's neck, or
When I held my H&K .45
To my next wife's head, or
When I destroyed my home
In front of my children…
Were You there?
Did You even care?

When I clenched my fists
And mutilated my face, or
When I held that same .45

Beneath my chin, or
When I shoved my Sister, and
Frightened my Mother...
Were You there?
Did You even care?

When I stood behind bars
Forced to sleep in a cage, or
When I screamed at my Father
Using Your name in vain, or
When I couldn't put down the bottle
And tried my hand with cocaine...
Were You there?
Did You even care?

Where are You now?
If there was ever a time, to
Show me You remember...
If there was ever a time, to
Show me I'm not forgotten...
If there was ever a time, to
Show me I'm on the right path...
This is the time

If You're there, You can see
My Soul is tired, so tired
Either bring me Home
Or guide my journey

My tears, dried
My lungs, opened wide
My shoulders, lighter
My stomach, void of nausea
My rage, now calm
My hate, now love

I heard Him speak
But not through ears, or
Even in my head, but
In my heart

"You are where I need you to be."
"You have always been where I need you to be."
"You are on the right path and I will guide you."

These words, if even words
Were spoken through my heart, and
Received by my Soul

My eyes gleamed
My smile true
My faith alive

He remembers
He has not forgotten
He has and forever will be
By my side

Only Three Weeks
Andrew R. Jones

It's just a day, well
Series of days, I guess
March 19 through April 8
Only three weeks if
Only three weeks

How long is only three weeks
When spent enduring gruesome combat?
Does it count as only three weeks?
Maybe three months or three years?

After Bootcamp you are a man… a Marine
After Infantry School you are a Grunt… a Warrior
What are you after combat?
More of a man? More of a Warrior?

To Marines yet to fight, a role model
A "Boot" who saw us as gods, he was
An odd Marine, but a Marine he was
It was in his name when stating
His rank and name, he followed with
"…as in, this Marine sure is odd"

He was eager to train and I was
Always harder on him, I ask
Myself these days, "Why?" I often
Wonder if I contributed to his instability
That day he opened fire on
His girlfriend's house saving the
Last bullet for himself

But back to the question
After combat, what are we?
Some say heroes even
That is debatable Achilles
Was considered a hero as well
As a brutal murderer

Does a Warrior cease to be a hero
When he returns and acts dishonorably?
Does he cease to be a hero
When he breaks and hurts innocence?

Then what is he?
A monster?
A beast?
An outrage?
An abomination?

I envy Warriors who died in battle
Forever Heroes buried with boots
Carefully pointed to 45 degrees
Service rifle standing covered
With an 8 pound Kevlar and a set
Of dog tags marking their eternal position

Only three weeks
It will pass just as
The last ten passed
I will survive just as
The last ten I survived

"And the gargoyles beheld wherever they roamed, that the souls of the lost weren't really alone. Each one had an angel, each one was protected, and each one was cherished and loved and respected."
-God Bless the Gargoyles by Dav Pilkey

Redemption
Andrew R Jones

We sit on opposite sides of a table in a back corner booth as Mom struggles to walk with the diner's famous apple pie.

"Where in the hell you been Aaron, and what's with that God awful smell all over you? You look like you haven't bathed in weeks."

"You're not looking so hot yourself. You come down with a fever?"

"It's nothing. I'm fine," says the little old Mexican woman as she walks away.

Mom isn't really my mom. I've been coming here since I was a teenager and even then, it seemed she had been a midnight waitress forever. I'm convinced the tips I've left over the years put her daughter through college.

She smelled of her usual generic perfume and the red-framed glasses covered half her face. Her step, a bit slower and strained. She coughs hard and immediately washes her hands behind the counter. I can't help but notice something isn't right with her.

"Aaron?"

"What?" Her voice brings me back to the table. I almost forgot she was sitting there.

"Your name's Aaron. Good to know. I had a cousin named Aaron. Lived on the Rez until he was 14. We had high hopes for him, but he stole his dad's truck one night and ran it into a pole. Crazy things happen out there. I stay in the city and go to school. You go to school? I think a higher education is important. My niece is 3 years old and loves kid's shows. Some of them are a little weird, but they help her along. I remember shows when we were kids..."

Here we go again. I've already begun to dig into the pie and if she doesn't do the same soon, I have no problem eating her half.

Finally Chamille takes a bite and tries to continue talking. It sounds like she mentioned something about penguins. I'm not sure. She continues to ramble on, but most of it comes across like Charlie Brown's mom, so I keep eating. After two weeks of starving my body, this pie has never tasted better. I'm sure later on I'll regret eating so quickly.

Later on.

Earlier I didn't have a later on.

On a concrete bench I sit as the moon glares from above--a spotlight for my performance. If all the world's a stage, this is my final act. Crickets supply an orchestra of the world's smallest violins, playing the world's saddest song. This bench is as cold as the death surrounding me. Rows of tombstones belonging to Warriors of the past line the grass fields.

I've performed the ceremonies and handed the Flag to loved ones of many of these fine men and women. Fear is nowhere to be found in my body because these dead are my friends. My brothers.

They are the ones who witnessed the end of war. Found peace. I envy them and choose to join their ranks this evening.

> Tonight, nightmares stop.
> Guilt subsides.
> Pain resolves.

Some people would suggest getting right with God or finding Jesus. Truth is, my faith in God is strong. After surviving Iraq, I felt He had a plan for me, or I was meant for something special. Turns out, He wasn't done laughing at me.

> For the last two weeks my taste buds felt only tears, whiskey and cocaine.
> *Two weeks.*
> Who survives for two weeks on whiskey and cocaine?
> *I do.*
> Why?

Because God refuses to take me home. He refuses to take away the pain and laughs as each disgraceful scene of this pitiful life plays out. Sympathy is not what I seek, so don't feel sorry for me.

> Redemption is what I claim tonight.
> For all the wrong I did to others.
> For all the pain I inflicted throughout the world.

"Wow," she says, "this is good. My grandma used to make the greatest apple pie."

For a brief moment I'm brought back to the diner. She continues to eat her share of the dessert and the silence pushes me back to an hour earlier.

I clutch the cold steel and find solace in knowing tonight, it's not up to Him.

Coyotes howl in the darkness, waiting for the trigger to pull; misunderstood creatures, not unlike myself. Once running with the wolves, but didn't have the stomach for ruthless killing. They try integrating with the dogs to find morality, but are shunned away and judged for where they came from. Caught in the middle to fend for themselves; resenting the dogs, but never returning to the wolves.

A breeze passes through, likely carrying the scent of sage and cactus. But I wouldn't know. Snot slides out of my nose and joins the tears running into my mouth. The last breeze I'll feel and I can't fully enjoy it. Taking a deep, burning drink of whiskey, I'm reminded of this pain being the only true and consistent part of my life.

My life.
If it even rates to be labeled a life.

A tragedy Shakespeare himself could not dream. Enough thinking. Time to take control and finish the scene.

Mom comes by and pours us fresh cups of coffee leaving the thermos at the table.

I collect my thoughts and return to the diner.

She begins to walk away, but Chamille's fork falls to the ground. She reaches to pick it up and Chamille places her hands around Mom's. An exchange of thoughts appears to occur as their eyes fixate on each other for several seconds. She releases and Mom smiles as she walks away. I take a look at Chamille and her eyes are still glossed over. Her hair still shines as it frames the edges of her face. She appears sad, but there's something more.

Something deeper.

A sadness originating from overwhelming love and compassion. Coughing hard again, Mom washes her hands and goes back to work. Chamille has become a little more interesting. I'm sitting here with this mysterious woman who appeared at my darkest moment and Mom, who appears to be in her dying days. Less than an hour ago I was fully committed to sending a .45 caliber bullet through my head.

My finger embraces the trigger as the barrel presses firmly beneath my chin. The hammer begins to click in preparation to strike the firing pin.

"Excuse me," says a voice from behind.

Sudden chill envelopes my body as a sense of panic sets in.
Who's behind me?
Does she have any idea my brains were about to be splattered in her general direction?

I slide the pistol into the front pocket of my hoody and try to figure out who this woman is and why she interrupted my final act. Before I can mutter a syllable--her voice takes over.

"I had no idea anyone else came here at night. I mean, who decides to spend their Friday night at a cemetery, right? I don't come here often, but when I do, I always find peace. Do you come here often? My Grandma is buried right over there. She died years ago, but I like talking to her. She always has the answers I need. When times are tough and..."

> Does she stop talking?
> Who is she?
> Where did she come from?
> I've been here for hours and haven't noticed a soul coming or going.

"...for some reason being here allows me to clear my mind. Maybe it's the music of the crickets or the howls of the coyotes. Such amazing animals. Anyway, so I told my sister he was going to be problems and..."

> Is this woman for real? Is this just another joke from God?
> Real funny.

I reach for my bottle but she finds it first. Oblivious I was also reaching, she takes in a mouthful of whiskey and sets it back down.

"Oh wow that burns. Then I was like, just drop the loser and focus on school..."

What else is she oblivious to? It doesn't seem she has any idea about my plan. She definitely isn't showing concern for my lack of participation in her rambling.

I decide to glance her way and look at what I'm dealing with. The moonlight displays her straight black hair and light brown complexion. Mexican or Indian, I'm not quite sure. There's a glare in her eyes and it's clear she's been crying. She's probably been here since the afternoon because it's cold, yet she only has a t-shirt on.

> Her voice is like... like...
> Beethoven on the piano.
> Michelangelo in the Sistine Chapel.
> A Spartan on the battlefield.
> Perfect.
> Flawless.

"...always had answers for me and told me what I should do. I always listen and on the most peaceful of nights I can hear her voice. Whispering and guiding me in the right direction, telling me there is rarely a right and wrong decision. 'There is no right or wrong,' she would say. 'There is just what you do and you do your best.' I always thought that was silly, but..."

I'm not sure what she's talking about. She could be reciting the multiplication table and I wouldn't care. I just want to hear her voice.

Tears flow from her dark brown eyes. She crosses her arms and shivers as her body reacts to the cold.

"Do you have any idea what it feels like to be so alone? To walk among people and to be in a crowd of your family and friends, yet you feel so alone?"

Her voice is shaky now. I nod my head ever so slightly, but can't bring myself to speak. I move the cold steel to my jeans pocket and without looking her way, remove my hoody and set it on her lap. She doesn't hesitate to put it on, letting the sleeves drape past her hands, keeping them warm. She sniffles and uses the cuff to wipe some tears away.

"...family doesn't understand. Friends don't understand. Only Grandma understands."
A moment of awkward silence begins.
She sniffles.
Crickets chirp.
Coyotes howl.
I pick at a scab on my hand.
Minutes pass and I break the silence.

"What's your name?"

"Chamille,"
"I was thinking about getting some pie."

"I'm starving."

I offer to drive and we make our way to my truck. The engine starts and the stereo blasts hard rock music I was listening to. She jumps at first, so I quickly turned it off. It's weird enough she accepted a ride from a stranger in the cemetery, so I don't want to make the situation any creepier. Surprisingly enough, she turns the music back on and it is the only noise as we cruise the dark roads to an all-night diner.

I give the occasional glance in her direction to make sure she is sitting there and--sure enough--she never disappeared. A couple of times I caught her doing the same. Was she wondering if I was real? Maybe she thinks she's dreaming. Maybe she finally realized how dangerous her choice to get into a drunken stranger's truck is. I don't know. I am actually hungry though--I know that.

The clanking of silverware brings me back to the diner as she continues to indulge in the pie.

"Do you like stories?" I ask.

She nods her head with intrigue in her eyes and takes another bite.

"One of my favorite stories is about the gargoyles." I say. "People once loved gargoyles and saw them as protectors. As time went on, the people forgot about them. Soon, they hated them. 'Grotesque creatures' they would say. 'Demons.' The gargoyles became sad. On rooftops they would sit and cry into the streets. Lonely and no longer needed. No longer wanted."

She kept her eye contact and I could tell she was interested.

"More tears flowed to the streets as they found themselves in their darkest moments. It was at that time; the Angels came down from the Heavens and sat with them."

The corners of her mouth slightly lift.

"Their pain began to diminish and a light of hope entered their souls. The gargoyles once again took flight into the night, always with an angel at their side and continued guarding the people."

"God Bless the Gargoyles. One of my favorite stories of all time," she says.

I can't believe she knows the story. She even knows the name. By this time she's pretty much finished the pie. I enjoy a few last bites and sip on my coffee.

Mom coughs.
Washes her hands.
Chamille sips on her coffee.
Dishes clank.
Food sizzles.
Fresh coffee drips.

"You ready to head back?"

She nods and wipes the coffee from her lips. I drop a $20 bill on the table and we begin to walk out. I push the door open looking back at Mom. I'm overwhelmed with a compulsion to wrap my arms around her.

So I do.

She squeezes me tight and I whisper in her ear, "I love you." She squeezes tighter just before letting me go and I walk out. Before the door closes I hear it.

She coughs.
She washes her hands.

With Chamille already in the passenger seat, I climb into my truck and start the engine. I want some time to process what went on in the diner, so I turn the stereo off and look at Chamille.

"Let's just keep it quiet for the drive back."

She nods her head and I pull onto the road. We arrive at the cemetery and I park in the same area as before. The moon continues to shine bright and I notice no other vehicles around.

"Where did you park?"

"I walked here this afternoon."

Paranoia is not a normal trait of mine, but the more I become comfortable with her, the more I want to fight it. We jump out of the truck and begin walking.

Not a word is spoken and I head for the Eternal Flame Memorial. It has a bright glowing flame promising to never burn out, in memory of the fallen Warriors. Chamille follows behind, almost guiding me to the flame. I feel its warmth as the glow reflects off my face.

"I know that feeling of loneliness. Every day since I came home 9 years ago. Left a hero. Returned a monster. 'You've changed' they tell me.

25

'What happened to the Aaron we used to know?' They couldn't understand anything I tried to explain. So I stopped. They weren't like me and I was no longer like them. I was alone."

After a couple of deep breaths, I hear only silence.

"Nightmares of graphic memories. Violent urges, some acted upon and others buried deep within. Guilt of my own survival. All for me to deal with. Alone."

She stands nearby, understanding there are no words for comfort. She places a hand on my shoulder and I feel hope. As much as I want to fight it... I can't.

"Innocent people died. Children died. My brothers died. Because of choices I made. For years I've asked God for forgiveness and for years I've been ignored. Left out in the cold to fend for myself. But tonight... tonight you changed that. I don't feel alone anymore. How? How did you change that?"

My eyes begin to water.

Her hand still on my shoulder.

I want to be mad at God for sending her to me. For giving me this hope I was so content on abandoning a few hours earlier. But I can't help but feel thankful.

I turn to give my gratitude.
But she's gone.
She's gone, but I'm not alone.
Hope radiates through my body
The sun begins to peek over the horizon.
A coyote howls in the distance.

I slide my hands into the warm pocket of the hoody, stroll back to my truck and drive home.

Cold Water, Sharp Blade

Andrew R. Jones

Cold water, sharp blade
Time to lie in the bed I've made

Warm whiskey, burning throat
No need to leave a note

Out of tears, out of time
Tired of being out of my mind

Deep breath, deep cut
Deep red flowing may it never shut

Down my arm, down the drain
Flow my guilt and pain

World fades, peace becomes
A sigh of relief understood by some…

★ ★ ★

Bright lights, loud beeps
Muffled voices, distant weeps

Death denied, pain returns
Thoughts of what I've learned

Not my choice, not my terms
No matter how I yearn

A purpose, a cause
A reason for my flaws

Whiskey, cocaine
Only mask the pain

Do you hear me? Do you care?
Or will you just continue to stare?

Wasted Words

Andrew R. Jones

A man racked the slide
The slide to his .45
Unable to set his guilt aside
He simply wanted to die

No more tears to cry
To cry for those who died
They say he was justified
Justified to end their lives

"It's war, it happens."
"You did the best you could."
"Life goes on."
"I'm sorry you had to go through that."
"It'll get better."

Wasted words in his mind
In his mind it's only lies
He called a guy
A guy who fought by his side
The guy heard not a word nor a cry
He hung up and rushed to his side

In a dark closet he did find
He did find the man with a .45
A bottle of whiskey at his side
The man still alive

They sat side by side
In the dark closet, no tears to cry
No telling how much time
How much time passed by

The .45 was handed to the guy
To the guy who said not a word by his side
This time he didn't die
He didn't die, but Death stood by

Day to day, lie to lie
Not a word nor a sigh to help him get by
Wasted words get lost and die
Get lost and die with those who reply

For those who cry
Who cry or want suicide
Sit by their side
In your silence they will confide

I Envy You
Andrew R Jones

Memorial for Staff Sgt James Cawley,
Platoon Sgt Fox Co 2/23. KIA Al Fajr, Iraq March 2003

You found rest
You found peace
I envy you

You perished on the battlefield
You no longer suffer
I envy you

You will not awaken to your own screams
You will not feel guilt in your dreams
You will not remember war at 19
I envy you

When in my darkest hour
When blinded from a flood of tears
When suffering consumes my body
I envy you

I am the cursed Warrior
The one waiting for the end of war
The one striving to be worthy of his sufferings

You are beloved Warriors, found your path Home
You are beloved Warriors, never to be left alone

You found rest
You found peace

I envy you

Forgiveness after the Explosion
Andrew R. Jones

Forgiveness, they say, is an action to benefit the one forgiving, not the forgiven. If this is true, then who is the beneficiary of forgiveness during a moment of self-forgiving? Through deep thought and logic, I obtained the ability to administer forgiveness to others.

> I delivered forgiveness to the soldier who attempted to deliver me death.

> As he battles insomnia, I wonder, does he observe me through the sites of his RPG?

> As he recalls our encounter, which emotion floods his body? Pride or remorse?

> As he centered an American Marine in his cross-hairs, what were his thoughts?

As the rocket impacted, did he smile?

As the shock wave carried my body, did he high-five the soldier beside him?

If he knew, I was still alive, would it anger him?

I have fantasized at times, of staring into his eyes and saying, "I'm still here motherfucker."

No. He is forgiven. Because he was doing what he was trained to do. I believe if I were to truly find myself in front of this man, I would stare into his eyes and firmly shake his hand. For on that day, in that moment, he was a better Warrior than I.

I made the call to forgive the Marine who made the call to fall back from our position, denying me the opportunity to respond with a rocket of my own. In the midst of confusion and an attempt to regain comprehension of the situation, I could not respond with as much as a middle finger while being assisted off the ground.

Forgiveness is given to this Marine because he made a decision which saved lives and prevented further injury. For in those moments of combat, a right or wrong decision does not exist. Only the decision which was made and you live with the knowledge you made the best decision you could.

With the logic gained during thoughts of the two previous recipients of my forgiveness, I realize only one person remains to be analyzed. Me.

Can I forgive myself?

On that day, I had served in the Marine Corps for three years, nine months and one day. I completed Marine Corps Recruit Training, The School of Infantry, advanced training schools as an Anti-Tank Assaultman, countless training missions and I proudly wore the stripes of a Corporal of Marines. I was, by definition, a Warrior forged in the fire of the most feared fighting force the present-day world knows to exist. Yet on that day, in that moment, my enemy was a better Warrior than I.

Eight Marines lined the rooftop, crouched behind a 3-foot wall. The Battle of Baghdad had commenced and casualties on all sides, civilian included, had been delivered. The rooftop was intended to provide us a tactical advantage to the urban battlefield. As I knelt behind the wall, my eyes panned the terrain, in search of a target.

Where were they?

Why was everything so quiet?

Hundreds of Warriors crammed into a city block and not one was pulling a trigger?

I continued my search, but was unsuccessful. If only the Iraqi could have said the same. A moment of calm confusion, instantly interrupted by what I can only describe as a tear in the very fabric of space-time. Time was described by Einstein not as a concept, but an actual physical entity of the dimensions of space. Just as the environment around us can be altered with mass and energy, so can time. As the rocket impacted, the explosion undoubtedly contained enough mass and energy to disrupt the space-time around me. Three chunks of wall floated through the air on my left. Islands amongst a sea of dust vividly engrained in my memory.

The Big Island of Hawaii occupied the position of top left, while Sicily and Okinawa followed below and to the right.

Bass rumbled through my head, not as a sound because my ears were rendered useless, but as an intense vibration.

> As time briefly came to a halt, my brain continued to produce thoughts.
> What the hell just happened?
> Where did that come from?
> Are the Marines beside me OK?
> Then nothing.
> Blackness.

To this day, I am uncertain as to how long my brain shut down in an emergency effort to protect itself. From what I am told, it was not too long. But how long is too long during an intense moment of combat?

As I returned to the sights and sounds of war, I was being lifted to my feet and told to fallback. During this moment, space-time realized I was caught in the earlier disruption and caused my environment to move at an incredible rate of speed, as if to, "catch me back up."

> Each day and night, this experience repeats in my mind.

> While driving.

> While eating.

CARDIFF
CAERDYDD

While chasing my children and flawlessly mimicking Donkey Kong.

To answer my earlier question, can I forgive myself?

Not yet.

I should have been better.

I should have been more vigilant.

I should have seen him if he saw me.

In time, I believe I will obtain the ability of self-forgiveness. I faithfully believe it is a pit-stop along this long treacherous road of healing I walk. Accompanied by my Brothers-in-Arms, I will continue to walk this road and pray the pit-stop is not much further.

Morning Thoughts
Andrew R Jones

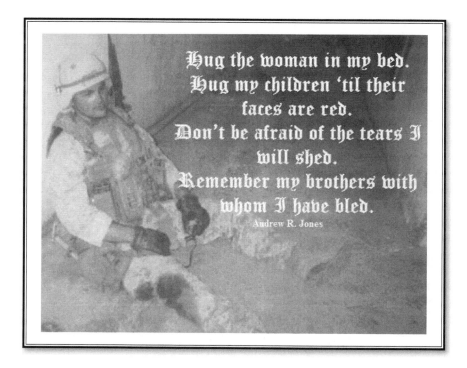

Hug the woman in my bed.
Hug my children 'til their
faces are red.
Don't be afraid of the tears I
will shed.
Remember my brothers with
whom I have bled.
Andrew R. Jones

Corporal Robert Jared McArthur after the
Battle of Baghdad, April 2003

Air raid siren
Body electrified
This isn't right

...There must be a mistake

The alarm is wrong
I fell asleep an hour ago
...Or was it three?

...There must be a mistake

Check the time
6am
Second opinion
6am

...There must be a mistake

Drape my arm across her body
Still here
Lost in dreams
Unaffected

...There must be a mistake

It's been two years
Free to leave
Life must be better elsewhere

...There must be a mistake

Kiss her neck
Squeeze her body
Roll to the edge of the bed

...There must be a mistake

My feet on the floor, I take a seated position
Followed by a silent cry of painful opposition
Back, knees, shoulders, hands
Reminders I'm alive, I should be ashes in the sand

...There must be a mistake

Death missed our appointment in Baghdad
Some would say I should be glad
He was a little busy that day
I was on his list he should have taken me, I say

...There must be a mistake

A prayer to God, His reminder I'm still here

...There must be a mistake

He never seems to care

A deep breath, stand on tired feet
A deep breath, walk to an aching beat

Granted another day to redeem my sins
Cursed another day to recall where I've been

...There must be a mistake

Maybe Death will realize his blunder tomorrow
Maybe he already has and enjoys my sorrow
Four thoughts are all I need
Four thoughts in my daily creed

Hug the woman in my bed
Hug my children 'til their faces are red
Don't be afraid of the tears I will shed
Remember my brothers with whom I have bled

The Calm
Andrew R. Jones

Amidst the calm
Sky is clear
Clouds moved on
But the storm rages on
Rages on amidst the calm

Amidst the calm
Rubble smokes
Heat is gone
But the fire rages on
Rages on amidst the calm

Amidst the calm
Air is still
Howling is gone
But the wind rages on
Rages on amidst the calm

Amidst the calm
Waves glide in
Caressing the sand along
But the water rages on
Rages on amidst the calm

Amidst the calm
Grass is soft
Mountains are strong
But the Earth rages on
Rages on amidst the calm

Amidst the calm
Explosions silence
Men's lives are gone
But the battle rages on
Rages on amidst the calm

Amidst the calm
All is well
We are where we belong
But the anger rages on
Rages on amidst the calm

Homage to My Hands
Andrew R Jones

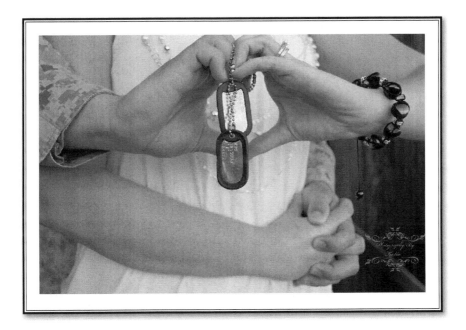

Photograph taken by Photography by Katie
www.photographybykatie09.wix.com/pbk09

These hands were strong hands
Longing for massive objects to lift
Solid walls or people to hit
These hands were strong hands
Uncontrollable in a rage of fit

These hands were strong hands
Doing as they may
Kept from fragile display
These hands were strong hands
Keeping evil at bay

Now these hands are scarred hands
Knuckles appearing to be bit
Exhausted and sick
Now these hands are scarred hands
Been through too much shit

Now these hands are scarred hands
"We're tired," they say
Stiff and in pain at the end of the day
Now these hands are scarred hands
Held together when I pray

These hands are loving hands
Lifting my children high
Caressing my fiancée at night
These hands are loving hands
Strong and scarred in all their might

The Bride

Andrew R. Jones

There's a story of a bride
A bride whose husband died
After the funeral she sat outside
Outside alone and cried
Loved ones offered their time
Their time at her side

"I'm sorry."
"If I can do anything to help, let me know."
"Call me if you need to talk."
"My prayers go out to you."
"Keep your head up."

To each she could not confide
Could not confide for her husband died
"Thank you," she replied
She replied, sat alone and cried

Along came a guy who sat by her side
Sat by her side, not a word nor a sigh
As the moon shined high
High in the sky
The guy remained silent
Silent at her side

He placed his hand by her eye
By her eye catching tears she cried
Her sadness she would no longer abide
No longer abide feeling hope and joy collide

She turned to thank the guy
The guy by her side
By her as she cried
"Where is he, did he hide?"
"He was here at my side."

She went to her husband
Her husband who died
Kissed his coffin, said goodbye
No words helped her get by
Just the guy
The guy with not a word nor a sigh

Under The Influence
(Drunken Thoughts of a Combat Veteran)
Andrew R. Jones

A man can have the greatest support group in the world.
But what good is that support group if the man won't reach out to it?
I want to be mad but at the same time I want to give in
Understand this is his choice in life.
I don't make his choices.
He does.

But is this a well informed decision?
Was he clear headed enough to make this decision on his own?
He just told me several months ago he was doing great.
He told me this as he was helping me through a hard time.

Did my questions make his situation worse?
Did it bring on guilt and the thoughts of whether or not he made the right decision?
Maybe it's a slow sadistic form of suicide?

Could he have those thoughts?
Wanting to die, but wanting to die painfully, slowly?
Pussies take a shotgun to their head.
Real men make it hurt.
They suffer. They witness
The destruction of their suicide as it happens.

Can a man be that sick?
Maybe this isn't what he wanted.
Like the man who jumps from a skyscraper and
Realizes half way down it was a shitty decision.
Too late.
But this is much slower.

We drink to numb the pain.
To make the pain go away, even just for a moment.
But it always comes back.
It lets you take your moment of solace and watches with a grin.
Knowing it will be back the next day and the day after that and the day
after that.
It laughs at your every attempt to get rid of it.
It's always there.
A part of you.

I hate you.
But you've done so much for me.
A punk kid turned into a Warrior.
You filled my head with thoughts of glory.
Thoughts of killing and how wonderful it is
But it's not.
It's gruesome.
It's tiresome.
It weighs on the mind.
It weighs on the soul.

You didn't promise me a rose garden.
You said it would be Hell.
But I had no idea what awaited me.
When you brought me out of my shell.

Everything you glorify,
Is everything that kills me now.
We were born in a bar and we drink to celebrate.
We scream kill and believe blood makes the grass grow.

I spent many days intoxicated in a war zone.
Thought it was a good thing.
Took the edge off.
Got me through the patrol, helped me sleep at night.

The Marine Corps is an obsession.
Worse than any obsession of love a man could feel for a woman
It continues to take from us.
It continues to feed off us.
And expects us to keep on giving.
To keep on sacrificing in its name.

But what do we get back from it?
A title?
A reputation?
Stories?
Memories?

It makes us think these are good things.
But in our society they are discouraged against.
Everything we are taught to love.
Everything we are taught to do.
Is discouraged in the society we are taught to do it for.

They hate us when we show them who we are.
They want us to fight for them and to kill for them.
But they can't stand who we are or what we do.

I hate you with the energy of a hundred suns.
But I love you with the passion of a hundred and one.
I gave you my life.

My Label
Andrew R. Jones

*Highway 7 near An Nasiriyah, Iraq, littered with the bodies of
enemy combatants and the civilian vehicles they used. March 2003.*

Post-Traumatic Stress Disorder, PTSD
This is the label stamped on me
Along with a mild Traumatic Brain Injury
Caused by the blast of an RPG

I began to ask, "What's wrong with me?"
I see what I have already seen
I hear screams which were already screamed
I bleed blood I should no longer bleed
What's wrong with me?

A disorder they tell me
A disassociation from society
A disagreement with how to be
A dysfunction with how I see
A disastrous monstrosity

No. Nothing is wrong with me
I am what I am meant to be
After experiencing war and tragedy
My actions should be labeled Normalcy

The Demon
Andrew R. Jones

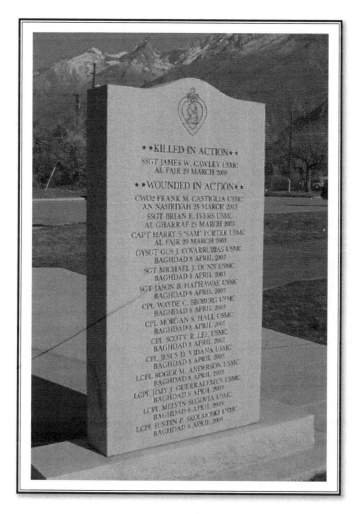

Demand of him, "Silence!"
He won't listen

Bind him to a chair
He won't stay

Secure him in a cage
He breaks free

Impale him through the chest
The blade fails

Shoot him in the face
The bullets bounce

Set fire to his body
He won't burn

Close your eyes, stay strong
He laughs and teases
Close your eyes, stay strong
Laughter ceases

Close your eyes, stay strong
He cries demon tears
Close your eyes, stay strong
He disappears

This battle you may claim
You live another day
Be grateful you get to stay
Remember those he took away

The Same
Andrew R. Jones

Private Andrew R. Jones alongside his Grandfather, Gunnery Sgt Charles Money, USMC Ret '53-'73 Korea and Vietnam. Taken October 1999

Our wars were different
Our questions the same
Did I make the right call?
Am I the one to blame?

We replay it in our dreams
We walk with guilt and shame
It rips at our souls
This demon of pain

We remember our brothers
May their sacrifice not be in vain
We live in their honor
Hoping peace will be obtained

Khe Sanh, Normandy, Inchon,
Baghdad, Kabul, La Drang
Our wars were different
Our tears the same.

REVEILLE

Andrew R. Jones

REVEILLE! REVEILLE! REVEILLE!
Up and at 'em Devil Dogs
Port side head, starboard side racks
Ready, MOVE!

Did you think the War was over
Because you came home?
Did you think you could drop your pack
Because you now feel alone?

On your feet Devil Dog!
FALL IN!
We're steppin' off in 5
Hydrate and pay attention.

Semper Fi, do or die!
Gung ho, gung ho!
What makes the grass grow?
Blood, blood, blood.

So take your Ka-Bar, with a Warrior thrust
Rip open your heart, feed your blood lust
Bleed onto paper, or into a megaphone
Leave no Marine behind, show we're not alone.

This is your voice, there are many like it
But this one is yours.
But your voice is only a tool, it is
A passionate heart which kills the
Stigma of our kind.
A passionate heart which kills the
Rep of the "Crazy Vet"

And what do we do for a living ladies?
KILL! KILL! KILL!

The deadliest weapon in the world is a
Marine and his HEART! It is
Your PASSION which must be harnessed if you
Are to survive this war at home.

Do not hesitate, do not procrastinate.
Fight with a happy heart and strong spirit
For we are told, "There is no better friend, no worse enemy
Than a United States Marine!"

We are told, "You are part of a brotherhood
From now on until the day you die,
WHEREVER you are, every
Marine is your brother."

WHEREVER we are.
Until the day we die.
"But I'm dead inside," you say.
"I'm here but my mind is there
So am I anywhere or am I everywhere?"
You ask.

Lace up your boots, follow me
Chest out, shoulders back
Reach out and touch
It's not time to hit the rack

Forward, STAND TALL
Forward, LEAN BACK
With a motivated heal stomp
KILL the depression
KILL the guilt
KILL the shame
KILL the rage
KILL the pain

Let the blood of our emotions
Flood the rivers of sadness so
They become a crimson tide
Of PASSION!

Let our voices boom above the masses
Because we are SHOCK TROOPS!
DEVIL DOGS! LEATHERNECKS!
We are motivated, we are strong!
We will no longer disassociate, we will belong.

We are surrounded by closed eyes
We are surrounded by closed minds.
Yes Chesty, that means those bastards can't get away now!
Once you are inspired to open your hearts
They will be inspired to open their eyes.

Do not fear your tears
Do not cower to judgment
We are here
Let's make it clear
This is our moment.

Dark
Andrew R Jones

It's dark.
No. It's beyond dark.
It's beyond any darkness I've ever experienced.
It's the complete and absolute absence of light.

I've been here before.
I can hear the screams as I move further into the darkness.
Women screaming in terror.
Children screaming in desperation.

But where are they? I can hear them but I can't find them. There's that smell again. I know that smell. It's such a unique and unmistakable stench.

It's the stench of flesh.
It's the stench of bodies being burned.

I see it now. I see the glow of the flames. The screams are becoming louder and more painful as I walk closer to the light. The dust clears and here I am again. I'm in the village now with the people. There is the woman in her black burka, kneeling over her young son. He lies there, wearing nothing but his torn up jeans. His chest is covered in gore and his skull and face are caved in and shine red. He lies there lifeless as the woman screams. She stops and turns my way.

Her black eyes glare deep into my soul.

She speaks in Arabic. I can't understand a word, but her tone tells me all I need to know. She blames me for this. She wants me to be the one death has taken, not her son.

"I'm sorry," I tell her, "I didn't mean to hurt your son."

More screams come from around the corner. Except these screams are unlike any I've ever heard. They are screams that instantly bring tears to my eyes and panic throughout my body. I race around the corner to help and there lying above a shiny red mangled women is a little boy. No more than 10 years old, in his torn t-shirt, jeans and bare feet. His hands are covered red. His cry says it all.

Why?
Why did they do this to you?
I love you! Don't leave me!
I walk over to comfort the boy.
"I'm sorry kid I didn't mean to hurt her."

He turns to me and glares with black eyes. I quickly try to escape around another corner and suddenly my feet are above me and I fall beside a large fire. Dust kicks up and the flames throw sparks at me. I look back to see what I tripped over and am overwhelmed with fear, guilt and panic. He lies there, still in his uniform. Wearing the green NBC suit over his desert cammies, flak jacket strapped on tight and M-16 at his side. But his face.

His face was ripped apart, deep red flowing into the dirt.

A familiar noise fills the air. What is that noise? That's right, it's me. This scream is my own. This shriek of terror and agony and guilt is that of my own doing.

"I'M SORRY!!! I'M SO SORRY!!!"

I look around and they begin to close in. The woman in the burka. The red-handed child. Now others. Men in Iraqi Republican Guard uniforms, ripped and stained red. They keep coming.

More deathly women and children.

Coming closer as they scream their hatred. I try to run, but as I turn there's only more horror behind me. A mountain of dead bodies piled up and ready to be added to the fire. I turn back and they're closer. I curl up in the dirt and close my eyes.

It's dark.
No. It's beyond dark.
It's beyond any darkness I've ever experienced.

We Burn the Fat off Our Souls

Adam J. Schirling

This is not a normal story, torn from the American History textbook of any high school that dots this country. We were a different group. We were not the heroic invaders, the conquerors tearing down the statues of dictators. Most of us were barely out of our teens when that happened. And we are not the last guys at the party, being shipped home now, nine years after the fact; met with parades and football games, and accolades. No, we weren't them either. We were the ones who went in between.

It was a cold January day in 2007 when I first stepped foot in Iraq. I was older than most in our company, a standard Marine Corps infantry company, but still younger than the older grizzled fucks who still remembered Bosnia and mid-90s booze cruises to the Med and South Pacific. I had spent seven months in late 2005 working in a trauma hospital in northern Kuwait, so I felt that gave me a level of cockiness that didn't reflect my actual experience. Sure, that 2005 deployment was full of horrific medical trauma on a daily basis, but I lived in a nice, air conditioned barracks that kept the desert heat at bay, and ate hearty meals at an Army chow hall, and watched movies at a makeshift theater. I knew nothing of actual war.

Stepping off that C-130 I did not know what to expect. There was not horrific bombing, nor bullet dodging. It was a quiet night, with a clear sky and shining stars. The smell, though, that was familiar. The smell of rotting garbage combined with diesel fuel and cooking fires, that was a smell I knew from the Middle East by this point in my young life. We boarded 7-Ton trucks, and drove to the main battalion camp, where we spent several days before being shipped out to combat outposts that dotted the battle space. My first outpost was a nice marble-lined house, with a spacious dirt yard. The sides were pockmarked with bullet holes and stains, and we dug piss tubes and built cardboard shithouses in the backyard. From there, a regimen of mounted and foot patrols commenced. I will not comment on the nature of most of these, out of respect for the men on them. We were there, and you were not, and therefore me telling you the nature of these excursions seems to me to be the same as showing a stranger my sister's diary. But with that said, there are memories that I will carry for our life.

There was the first Iraqi house I ever stepped foot in. My platoon commander and a squad embarked on a foot patrol one night, and stopped at a house to question the occupants. I remember the apprehension on the man's face at the door, and the fear of the children who peeked from the corner as the host served us chai tea and bread. My heart wrenched at these dirty, fearful kids. As a young father of an infant, my heart leaped at the sight of scared toddlers. This was not a sentiment shared by my compatriots, as they were mostly in teens, and without child. That night I gave them candy, and my heart was warmed by the happy giggling of the little fuckers as I handed them a handful of Jolly Ranchers I had stuffed in my pocket before leaving the outpost. After that night I never left the outpost without a pocket full of candy to hand the kids. When I close my eyes now, I see most of them, annoying little bastards that they were, and wonder how many of them are now dead. I suppose great deals of them are, but some remain, and I wonder if they remember Jolly Ranchers and a large sweaty man who pitied them.

The days blur together from that deployment. Moments of hilarity and long expanses of boredom broken by short moments of sheer terror mixed with excitement. Long hot days, sand storms and sudden rain downpours, Shitting in Wag bags and treating all the bumps and bruises and illnesses of a Marine grunt unit, I was a 23 year old Corpsman, in charge of nine other young Corpsmen, who were responsible for all the routine and traumatic medical needs of 179 U.S. Marines who were engaged in direct combat daily, five hours from the nearest hospital. To be a Corpsman during wartime in a Marine grunt unit is a very unique part of US military history. We are part paramedic, part doctor, part nurse, part counselor, part medical administrator, and part grunt. I cut warts off cocks, treated diarrhea, and patched bleeding wounds. I yelled about hand washing and made sure the shit was being burned properly. And I loved every minute of it.

Bishop caught a bullet in the chest one day. He was a veteran of numerous deployments, in a semi-safe area, and well-liked by many. He choked to death on his own blood while enroute to a trauma hospital. I still see him when I close my eyes, his Tennessee accent and funny grin while he told stories of drunken one-night stands and favorite bands. He was a good friend, and his death was taken hard by the men. I pray one day I can see his grave, and be able to close my eyes and see my friend again, happy and grinning.

That deployment was followed by another one seven months after returning home. This one was a bit safer, as it was now a year later in the war, and Fallujah was about as dangerous as South Central L.A. in the way that it was now familiar and normal, but danger still lurked around every corner, and death struck when no one expected, in horrible ways. A young Marine was executed while on post at a very small combat outpost, the motherfucker snuck into the wire and shot him in the back of the head while he manned his machine gun in the middle of the warm Arabian night, probably thinking of his girlfriend and beers back home with his bros. I don't remember his name anymore, and that bothers me very much. I remember when his killer was captured, I did his confinement physical before he was shipped to prison, and I don't know what happened to him either, and I wish I did. I hope he was executed, but most likely not.

Shortly after I returned home from that second Iraq deployment, combat operations in Iraq were announced to be over, and a smaller force of 'advisors' were left in our place, while attention was switched to Afghanistan, which had begun to heat up once again. I was slated for a fourth deployment, but due to the demands of a selfish wife, I transferred to an administrative job; watching my friends and brothers leave without me. That has haunted me more than anything in the world, still to this day. Hearing of my friends fighting and dying while I drank beer and played with my kids and watched reality TV fills me with a void of shame and agony that cannot be described. And I suspect that is a feeling shared with many of my brothers who left the service, regardless of the year. To be a former warrior is a hard task. To know you are safe and warm when men wearing your colors and crest, and fighting and crying, and dying in the blood of a foreign land, is a very fucking hard thing to accept. Whether you do four years or 20, a TRUE warrior has a hard time setting down his weapon and adopting a life of domestic tranquility and peace. He will never forget being a warrior, and knowing what it is to be cold, and scared, and hungry; no matter how much success he achieves or how long his beard grows and his waist expands.

I miss my war. I miss my friends. They are scattered, these days, all over the globe. Some are still Marines, and are in Afghanistan as I am writing this. Some have become private contractors, still wishing that warrior lifestyle but with a higher paycheck. And the majority of us are home now. We are safe, and happy, with children and wives. For many of us it is our 2nd, or 3rd, or 4th wife; as the life of a warrior is a demanding one and many women cannot meet the challenges of a warrior's wife. And a horribly high number of us are dead. The ones that did not fall in combat died in suicides, and traumatic accidents, and sudden illness. In fact, more of my friends have met death after returning from war than those that met it in direct combat. It is a haunting revelation. It sometimes feels as though we are all marked somehow. We dared and defied death so much for so long, that he came looking for us when we are home and vulnerable. That a witch now follows us, hides in the shadows, striking when least expected. In that dim twilight of senses before I fall asleep, I sometimes see that witch, a dark cloud of energy, and am terrified for when the day arrives that she comes for me, striking when I am happy and weak. I hope that she forgets me, but I know she will remember one day.

I miss my rifle. I miss my pack. I miss my boots. I miss my brothers. Nothing remains for us now; just babies and memories, dreams and smells, graves and job interviews. When I drink a bit too much, the sights and smells come flooding back. The faces and laughter of dead friends fill my ears. The feeling that no matter what, we did right in the world and we somehow mattered despite our middle child sentence of this war.

When I look at the news today, surrounded by my family and my chin long with beard, and hear the war in Iraq is officially over, I am saddened when I realize the war in Iraq has been over for my friends and me for quite some time now. But at the same time, it will never really be over, because we were young and foolish and brave, and when we close our eyes for the last time, whether it is 50 years from now, or 5 days, we will remember that we were part of history. We fought and laughed and cried, and did our best with the cards we were dealt. And that is all that can be asked of any group of warriors. We were the ones who came in between. And we forged a legacy of honor that will resonate through history, not for horrific casualties dealt to our fathers and grandfathers, but rather our willingness to stand and fight when so many of our peers would not. That is our legacy; and we will carry it until the end of time.

If you see an Iraq vet on the street, just shake his hand. Or do not. But remember in your heart what he did, at a time before recessions and Marjah; a time before military downsizing and forced early outs. Remember he stood up, and asked to go where so many Americans were being slaughtered, when 99% of his peers would not. Remember that one percent.

Old Friends
Adam J. Schirling

"They were standing right there, right next to me," I stood and screamed this to the bar. "Where the hell did they go?"

I stumbled off my barstool, my head snapped around in disbelief. One minute we were hanging out and drinking beers, I turn my head to scan the beautiful ass of a college chick wearing far too short of denim shorts, and when I turned around, nothing. All gone. I grabbed the waitress, fear in my eyes, dripping into my voice. I asked her where my friends went. Quivering with fear, noticing my large size and tattoos, she tearfully told me she didn't know.

Panic filled my heart. Thick, salty tears rolled down my face, into my greasy matted beard. I was beyond insane now. Breaths were heavy, senses extended to the point of super-human levels. I strained these new super-senses to catch any evidence of my friends. They were supposed to be my closest friends. I busted into the street screaming names into the cold wet air. A heavy hand landed on my shoulder. I turned ready to attack, but saw the giant frame of the bar manager, Ryan.

"Listen dude," he said, "get back inside and calm down and we will find your friends."

His statement, while polite and nearly friendly, left no room for insubordination. Still crying, I walked into the bar and sat at the stool; ashamed and embarrassed.

WHY, WHY, WHY, WHY, is all I could think.

Why would they ditch me like that? We were the closest friends. The problem plagued me, making me sick, and I felt on the verge of another meltdown. Instead, I meekly had the bartender, and old high school basketball team mate, bring me whiskey straight.

I was so happy when the guys came out to the worksite. Surprised me out of the blue, it was the greatest of reunions. The day cutting lumber in the Pacific Northwest left me exhausted, but seeing the smiling faces of the guys gave me a jolt of instant energy.

We piled into my old '55 Chevy pickup and cruised the summer highways; laughing and drinking beers, basking in the glory of youth and twilight through the redwood trees. We decided to pull into the Redneck Roadstop, a joint where I knew we could drink beer, play pool, flirt with cute community college chicks, and get a little twisted. The regulars there would accept my friends; they have certainly earned their right to booze and partake in tomfoolery at such an esteemed location.

But it went terribly wrong. I just couldn't see them betraying me for a joke; we have been through too much. The tears came back, soft sobs as I buried my head in the bar.

"I don't get it," the waitress said to the bartender. "What is he freaking out about? Who the hell is he looking for?"

"You will see in a few minutes, girl. And it won't be pretty. This happens about once a month and it tears me up to see every time."

The police strolled in and sat beside me at the bar.

"Hey, son. How you doing tonight?" the big one, clearly in charge asks me. "They say you have a missing group. Maybe we can help. Give us their names and info, and we will if we can't turn them up, OK?"

His voice was comforting and I nodded slowly.

"Please just find my friends," I pleaded softly.

After about 25 minutes, the cop came into the bar, sat next to me and ordered a local draft.

"Well, Val, we found your friends. 'Toby' or more actually Lance Corporal Tobias Jackson was killed in Action November 12 in Fallujah, Iraq. 'Nick' or Lance Corporal Nicholas Anderson killed in Action November 15 in Fallujah, Iraq. And 'Stan" or Sergeant Stanley Moreau committed suicide three weeks after they got back from that deployment. But you know that, Val, because you were there for all them to die. You saw it with your own eyes; the life spill out onto the sands. So they aren't here with you tonight."

My mind exploded in flashes of red and yellow. A scream unleashed from my throat like an animal of the very depths of Hell. I shot up screaming in disbelief, calling them all liars, before throwing my beer bottle against the grown and storming out yelling insane babbles into the dark night.

The bartender went to the cop, and saw tears streaming from behind his glasses.

"That's the 3rd time this month, Sherriff. When he comes in smiling saying his friend are with him, we just give him the farthest booth and hope he stays quiet."

The Sherriff's shoulders shook with the sobs.

"I don't know why my boy sees them, he just does. He is supposed to go talk to the shrinks at the VA, but he refuses."

The cop got up with a sigh, and went into the night in search of his son, who is most likely naked in a tree by now, with handfuls of drugs.

The bartender locked the door and hit the lights as he walked away. Closed for the night. The last thing seen by both men driving out of the lot is the American Flag flying above the door.

I'm There Now
Cleo Riley
04-21-02

Blazing sun, and dirty streets,
Starving kids with nothing to eat.
Diseased water and adults too.
No electric, or money, just an ocean of blue.

Death lingers in the air.
The stench of blood, and I don't care.

I'm there now, and nobody knows.
In my mind where memories flow.

I stare off into the distance, lost in thought.
Thinking of a foreign land, where I once fought.
Where Soldiers fell, and lost their lives.

Far away from their children and wives.
It was nine years ago that I was there.
Until I get lost in that distant stare.
It was yesterday, today, tomorrow, and forever.
When will I come home? I think never.

I'm there now, and nobody knows.
Attacked by memories that constantly flow.

The look in their eyes, to this day still haunts me.
Invading my sleep, they always taunt me.
I fought them once, over there.
They followed me? Is that fair?
I can hear them, smell them, all around.
But I don't see them, can they be found?
Maybe they're hiding under my bed.
They seem so close, are they in my head?
I open my eyes and jump to my feet.
Reaching for my weapon, me they won't defeat.
My weapon is gone, it's not there.
Neither are they, I was just lost in a stare.

I'm there now, and nobody knows.
I can't breathe when the memories flow.

Jesus and the Soldier
Cleo Riley
09-24-09

I have walked miles and my sandals are dusty.
I have walked through the desert and my boots are dusty.
I wore a crown of thorns as the blood dripped down my face.
I wore a helmet as the sweat dripped down my face.
The cross I carried on my back was heavy.
The pack I carried on my back was heavy.
The people threw stones at me and cursed me.
The people shot at me and screamed.
I hung on the cross and died for your sins.
I jumped on a grenade and died for my friends.
I gave my life for the world.
I gave my life for my country.
People worship me now.
People cry for me now.
You have earned a place in heaven.
You have earned a place in my heart.
You are now my child.
You have always been my Father.

The Hands
Richard Brewer (Founder of One Warrior Won)

The hands that were once used as a pacifier for a new born child
The hands that were used to reach out to hold my mother's legs
The hands that were held by my parents to ensure I stay close by
The hands that awkwardly wrote that first love note in third grade
The hands that were used as a teenager to prove my self-worth
The hands that reached out and held my first girlfriend
The hands that struggled to break away from ordinary and reached
for extraordinary

These were the hands that rose and swore to defend this nation from the enemy; foreign and domestic.

These were the hands that nervously grasped the stair rails of a bus bound for Parris Island in the middle of the night.

These were the hands that were held tight to the seams of my "trousers" while being screamed at standing on yellow footprints

These were the hands that climbed obstacles they never thought possible, that learned to defend for the righteous

These were the hands that first felt the cold comfortable steel of my newly issued M16A1 service rifle

These were the hands that spent weeks feeling, touching, learning every part of the very weapon that was to keep me and others alive

These were hands that proudly had the Eagle, Globe and Anchor pressed into its palm transforming from a mere mortal to a Marine.

These were the hands that committed to God, Country, and Corps

These were the hands that embraced the brotherhood that has been bonded by blood, sweat and tears.

These were the hands that grasped the seat of the swaying Chinook as it took evasive action while delivering us to the hostile shores.

These were the hands that held firm, aimed true and gently squeezed the trigger to silence a different set of hands that will forever remain unknown

These were the hands that steadied scared people as they were gently pushed to waiting choppers to carry them from the surreal reality of war to safety

These were the hands that held the head of youth, shattered by a snipers bullet, providing comfort awaiting the last breathe

These were the hands that held my own head down in holes never deep enough as the rounds pounded way to close

These were the hands that waved good-bye to thousands of Marines as they sailed away from the hostile shore

These were the hands that grasped tightly to the fourteen Marines left behind to guard the bees' nest that had been vigorously stirred

These were the hands that clasped tightly every night in prayer to preserve my life until I woke, and again in the morning to pray to survive the day.

These were the hands that waved frantically to my office colleagues to take cover as I grabbed my weapon and ran towards the noise

These were the hands that reached for that sliding glass door that allowed me to step onto the exposed balcony

These were the hands that attempted to hold steady the weapon I knew so well, only to have it blown from my hands by the force of the bomb

These were the hands that flew through the air for untold feet only to crash against the collapsing wall.

These were the hands that were buried and felt my own body to see if it was in one piece

These were the hands that scratched, clawed, and dug my way out from what I believed to be a premature coffin, only to hear and see the hell unfolding around me and wanting to crawl back into my hole

These were the hands that would hold the soon to be lifeless bodies of two close buddies trying to make their last moments less lonely

These were the hands that would dig, uncover and carry untold numbers from the burning and destroyed building

These were the hands that again took hold of my precious weapon and stood guard against a secondary attack

These were the hands that held my body off the ground as I fell to my knees, not knowing why until it was realized the blood covering me was my own

These were the hands that shakily signed me out of a field hospital to return to the pile of flesh infested rumble

These were the hands that stood guard over the ground that only mere moments ago stood the American Embassy for four sleepless days

These were the hands that wiped away dust from my eyes and wished for the tears that never came to flow

These are the hands that now try to hold a fragile life and family together

These are the hands now that try to hold a beast within at bay

These are the hands today that hold a wonderful wife

These are the hands that two young children rush to for safety and love

These are the hands that have tried to teach young minds the perils and purpose of war

These are the hands that have provided protection to communities from those who wish them harm

These are the hands that have shied from friendship for fear of being exposed

These are the hands that are never idle in fear of some distant unseen enemy

These are the hands that for years never reached out, stoically staying by my side

These are the hands that wrapped themselves around a bottle, the only medicine able to take the unseen but always present pain away

These are the hands that hide the scars that so many do not wish to see, yet so many of us bear

These are the hands that have reached out after 25 years for help, and were slapped by those professing to be helpers

These are the hands that had to enter battle all over again simply to be recognized as worthy of treatment and care

These are the hands that have been clasped together in prayer for someone to understand

These are the hands that have been clenched in anger over those who have never served making us prove we indeed did serve

These are the hands that have flailed about speaking jargon others seem to think is a foreign language

These are the hands that have spent countless hours typing rebuttals to the appeals of my appeals

These are the hands that have fantasized about being around the neck of so many who say they are there to help, but never do

These are the hands that have been thrown in the air, and wishing to wash themselves of the entire process

These are the hands that have written farewell notes to loved ones; too tired to go on

These are the hands that have tried to write, hoping to get someone to see what I feel

These are the hands that have grasped the cold comfortable steel of an old trusted friend in hopes of ending the pain and suffering

These are the hands that held a family vacation itinerary in one hand, and the end in the other

These are the hands that God made and Parris Island perfected

These are the hands that have saved so many, and protected so much

These are the hands that have lost battles, but will eventually win the War.

These are the hands that remain clasped in prayer every night, praying that justice will prevail for me, and all who suffer from the beast within.

These hands paid a dear price for this country. Now it is time for this country to pay a little back.

All gave some; some gave all. What has the country given to them?

Sinister Rage

Joseph A. Bales

A sinister rage grabs hold
I cannot fight this
Swirling in a symphony
Of evil pleasure

I hear the rounds
Ping… ping…I laugh
"Sabot out," my enemy breathes his last
His children will fight me in coming years
I am fine with that

House to house we watched the enemy fall
With an, "On the way…" a vivid painting on the wall
One by one, wave after wave
They hit the dirt in the same gruesome way

Until we hear, "Halt!"
We won't stop the slaughter
Cry Havoc! The tempo grows hotter

On day three of no sleep we start to wonder
What is real and what is fake we ponder

A quick nap, back in the fight
Living boyish dreams of glory and might

Yet atop our throne of heartless steel
We see something that makes us feel

A young child walks to our beast, unafraid
Arms outstretched, Death has not made

We stop for a moment as the universe shifts
From raging inferno to a nicer death pit

An impact brings us back to life
Back to the paradise some would call strife

When the battle is over,
The smoke has cleared
We will smile and know,
Forever we will be here

Split Second
Linda Eden

Split Second Transgression
Eternal Damnation
Perfection obliterated
Reverse! Reverse!
The hands of time.
I'd give these hands of mine -
would give all!
For the split second behind.

Declaration of War
Jenn Merriman

Photo taken by Lorilei Nash with Siren and The Machine Photography
www.facebook.com/sirenandthemachinephotography

July 4, 2012

Dear PTSD,

I didn't know much about you in the fall of 2008. I didn't hear the rumors or the horror stories; you were more of an unspoken evil that was frowned upon. I knew when my fiancé came home from war he'd be different. A deployment would change him, a death of his friend would change him. But that was ok because we loved each other and I was going to be standing by his side to support him.

He would have his moments of remembering his fallen friend's death anniversary and those days were hard for him. Memories and nightmares of being deployed, but I was there to stand beside him and help him get through it. We were doing well; he seemed to be doing well also. One night all of a sudden, yes PTSD I'm talking to you, you reared up, sleeping dormant for a few years, and his true feelings about his friend's death came out. He wished he was dead and could trade places. That night I had to hide all the weapons in the house and I didn't sleep at all, checking on him all night to make sure he didn't leave or find the weapons I had hidden. Still didn't know what you really were PTSD. I didn't understand yet.

This wasn't enough for you yet. We got engaged and were very happy, the happiest day of our lives, we were planning our future together and it was amazing. We loved each other, been through so much together and our relationship had only grown stronger. We felt invincible. Then PTSD, you decided to make it where he couldn't fight against you anymore. He had been protecting me from you for so long, I had no idea who you were or what you were capable of.

After Christmas and the first of the year, you decided to break my fiancé down where he couldn't fight you off anymore. You broke his heart and his spirit. You forced him to shut off his emotions, stop caring about himself or anyone else. He hates himself, isn't capable of loving. You forced him to drink more to cope with your nightmares. You made him paranoid that he was back overseas; his head is there because of you. You forced him to push everyone away. PTSD, your effects weren't only on him, you tried to make me give up on him. Question my trust and love in him. You made me confused, hurt, at my lowest you made me want to die because I didn't understand the terror you had created on my fiancé. I didn't realize what he was going through was your doing. Not how he really felt and not what he really wanted. Yes PTSD, you tried to get me to stop loving him, but guess what? I have your number now PTSD! I now realize what your game is and what you are trying to do to my fiancé, myself, and our families. It's not going to work; I will not give up this fight to you! You tried to not only kill him, but you tried to make me doubt our love for each other and the strength of our relationship. You made me believe that this was my fault and that I'm an awful person and I don't deserve to be alive anymore. You have tortured my fiancé, made him a shell of himself. He's cold inside. He feels empty and shut off. He only wants his space, and I can't do something as simple as hug him to make him feel better. He wants no touch or human contact. You've made him not trust anyone, you've made his thoughts all over the place and not rational. PTSD, you have gone so far as to make him wish he was dead. And now you've tricked him into believing he doesn't need help. At least not yet.

PTSD, I will not give up this fight! I will not stop loving him because you are having fun wreaking havoc on the love of my life! I will not give up on him, on our relationship, on our future together! I will keep learning about you and your dirty tricks you play! I will be there, standing with my hand out stretched to my fiancé to help pull him out of your awful grasps! I will not go away! My fiancé and I will beat you, we will defeat you, and our relationship will grow stronger! You might have your infected claws in him right now, but I will not give up this fight, I will help him pull out every last claw you stuck in his body and mind!

PTSD, please take this as a declaration of war, from a girl that loves her fiancé more than you can imagine and has more fight in her than you know. You might have won this battle, but you will not win the war! I will help him free himself from your enslavement. This is my declaration of war on you PTSD!

Sincerely,

The girl who won't give up...

A Soldier's Wife
Deborah Leblanc

Photograph taken by Photography by Katie
www.photographybykatie09.wix.com/pbk09

I am a soldier's wife, loving and proud
I stand with many and pray out loud
You are my hero, my husband, my friend.
I promise to stand strong till you are home again.

Sometimes I get weary in the middle of the night,
I hold your pillow... oh so tight
The tears, they come, the rivers they flow
but I understand truly deep within my soul.

Your job is important, duty calls
You are a soldier standing tall
Fight the good fight, finish with faith
and know at home, I will await

I love you my soldier, so strong and true
One day soon, we'll be together...
Me and you.

A Year

Deborah Leblanc

What a year this has been,
A year of fears and new friends
Facebook, Skype, text messages abound
Words of encouragement when we were down

For on that day when our soldiers left,
We wept many tears and asked ourselves,
"What will we do, how will we survive
with this empty hole left within our life?"

We clung to our cellphones
Our computers always charged
From lines of communication
We didn't stray far

Waiting and watching
Checking all the time
Just to see if our soldier
Had made it online

Care packages and pictures
Paintings and gifts
We sent to our soldiers
No week did we miss

Our soldiers fought long
Our soldiers fought hard
Messages were sent
Of news from afar

Family and friends this year has been long
But now our soldiers have made their way home
Let us not forget as we return to our lives
The 926th family that helped us survive.

With Love to ALL

Mission Accomplished
Deborah Leblanc

Photo taken by Lorilei Nash with Siren and The Machine Photography
www.facebook.com/sirenandthemachinephotography

Your love for your God, Country, Family and Friends
Took you to places we cannot comprehend.
You dedicated your life and took the oath
To defend us all with your very soul.

Many do not understand why you chose this path
To leave everyone and travel the map.
Across the miles, the loneliness abounds
As you lay in trenches and hide behind mounds.

You fought for freedom, defended the land
You saw many horrors, long days without end.
Now it's time to come home, your mission is done
A new day begins with the rising of the sun.

Thoughts cross your mind as you make your way back
Will everyone still want me, how will they act?
Will I be able to deal with the pressures of life
Since I've seen such turmoil and strife?

Soldier, know there were many who prayed
Preparations made with each passing day.
Acts of love by your family and friends
Since the day you left till you return once again.

We love you, we thank you, the pride in our hearts
Grew stronger each day that we were apart.
Lay down your pack, lay down your gun
Welcome Home SOLDIER, your mission is done.

'Twas the Night before Reunion
Deborah Leblanc

Photograph taken by Photography by Katie
www.photographybykatie09.wix.com/pbk09

'Twas the night before Reunion, when all through the town
Every household was stirring, they could not settle down

The kitchens were mopped and the floors swept clear
Knowing our soldiers would soon be here

The children were all wrestled quickly to bed
While visions of camouflage danced in their heads

And mamma in her curlers with a mask on her face
Tried to relax before the big day took place

Out on the lawn there stood a big sign
Shouting to neighbors, "Once again he is mine!"

We tossed and we turned all night through
Thinking how this deployment made us more true

The friends we have made and the bonds we did form
Gave us the strength to be there Saturday morn

When, what to our wondering eyes did appear
But a chartered airplane and all of their gear

With a pilot so proud to carry them in
We knew in a moment it must be our men

More rapid than eagles our soldiers they came
As we cried and cheered, yelling out their names

All parents, all children, all spouses and friends
Jumping and leaping as the plane came in

Reporters with cameras stood there in awe
What a wonder to behold the sight they saw

As the flags began to wave, the confetti began to fly
Everyone stood proudly, holding up their signs

The plane wheels hit the tarmac and came to a halt
The engines stopped turning, we all began to shout

And then all of a sudden the door opened wide
There stood the first soldier, gleaming with pride

As the welcome party gathered around
They quickly descended the steps to the ground

Though dressed in uniform from covers to boots
Not a moment did it take to know who was who

All eyes-how they twinkled the smiles how merry
The tears how they flowed, noses red like a berry

Everyone gathered, children in tow
Welcoming our soldiers and happy to know

All the worried days and all the lonely weeks
Were now really over, as we stood cheek to cheek

The deployment was over, everything ended well
All our worries laid to rest, memories placed on shelves

Balloons were released and speeches were read
The ceremony then ended and farewells were said
We sprang to our cars amidst the hustle and bustle
And away we all flew, no more thoughts to struggle

And we heard Baton Rouge exclaim, as we drove out of sight
Welcome Home Soldier, Have a Blessed Life

I am the Wife of a United States Marine
Lisa Spencer

Lisa and Jason Spencer at the Marine Corps Ball.

This gives me immense pride to say. We were married June 16, 2001; three months before the horrific terrorist attacks of 9/11 completely changed our lives. On our wedding day I was so proud to walk down the aisle to my Marine in his Dress Blues. I was proud to stand for pictures in my white wedding dress surrounded by Marines in their Dress Blues. I loved the ceremony where I was whacked on the bottom with an NCO sword as my official "Welcome to the Corps!" That day was all finery and show. Our families were beaming too. I was proud that night to feel my Marines' arms around me and his kiss and the power of his love for me. On that night, we had no idea, in three months, our lives would change forever as America was forever scarred.

On 9/11 we didn't panic, we sat and watched the nation we love be attacked. We watched Americans jump to their deaths rather than being burned alive. We were saddened and angry, but we knew this meant war. Who craves war more than a Marine Corps Infantryman? My heart sank as I came to realize the day my husband would be deployed to retaliate for these acts of terrorism. But as quickly as it sank, it swelled with pride. I was proud I was married to a man who volunteered to serve his country, and I was proud he was going to be a part of the "War on Terror."

In 2005, his turn came, leaving our home with me and our three children ages two, seven, and nine and went to do what he had trained for years to do. He was calm. He reassured me he would do everything he could to come home to us, but he wasn't scared. He didn't say goodbye, he said "See you later," then turned and walked away.

That deployment was difficult to say the least. Forty-eight members of his unit paid the ultimate price for our freedom. It was hard to see another casualty on the news and then wait. It was either a knock on the door or a phone call. Phone calls were good because it was always him telling me he was ok. Every time I heard his voice on the line, I would breathe a huge sigh of relief that he was alive, and then my heart would break because I knew another family was getting a knock on their door.

I would always say to him, "Just come home! Just come home to me and everything will be OK." I didn't contemplate he would be a different person when he came home. I didn't care. I just wanted my husband back.

He made it! It was so good to hear his voice on the phone and know he was on American soil. I was so happy, tears streamed down my face. He was in North Carolina at Camp Lejune, and he would be allowed to return home to Ohio in about a week. He wanted me to come see him in North Carolina, so I arranged a babysitter and drove the 14 hours to see him. I threw the car in park and didn't even close the door. I saw him standing on the second floor balcony of a hotel and ran to him. I imagined this moment every day and night of the deployment. I imagined he would embrace me and pick me up and twirl me around and kiss me and we would both cry tears of joy. That didn't happen. I ran into him so hard it made him take a step back. He put his arms around me and buried his face in my neck and just took several deep breaths. I pulled back and looked at his face and his eyes were different, darker, almost haunted. He said, "Hey, good to see you." In that moment, our new reality began. Our new reality was life with PTSD. We didn't know it yet, we just knew things were different.

Over the next few years, I became used to the excessive night sweats, night terrors, increased startle reflex, bursts of anger, bouts of deep sadness, depression even crept in a few times for both of us. I, as many civilians and others who don't understand PTSD, came to think this is what PTSD is. I have come to understand it is the very tip of a gigantic iceberg. It has taken me years to get where I am. And I have not done so without making many mistakes. I have judged my husband and hurt him deeply by doing so. I have made him feel that I expect an end to PTSD, that somewhere out there, there is a cure, and if I do enough research, and cart him to enough counseling sessions, he will have an epiphany and be healed. I could feel he was holding me at arms' length and I started to think something was wrong with me. I didn't realize that I was the one who needed the epiphany. It took almost losing our marriage and knowing if our marriage ended, he would most likely end his life, to get me really digging deep and finally coming to comprehend what my husband lives with every day. Every minute of every day of every year of his life, he deals with the torture that is PTSD.

Sure, there is the "hyper-vigilance" (which he calls "situational awareness"), the startle reflex, night sweats, night terrors, sadness and depression which is always grasping at him and wanting to take more and more of him away. Physical pain accompanying depression makes things he used to enjoy impossible, which in turn, worsens his depression. There are friends lost because they don't understand him anymore. There are people offended by outbursts of anger. There are those horrified by stories he finds amusing. There are issues with his memory. Issues he comes across while driving. Issues with being confined. Issues with being in large crowds. Issues with being in small crowds. I could go on and on, but these are all surface issues. These are things people can notice about him which are different than he was before the deployment.

As his wife, I noticed more. And come to realize the "more" is the real problem. I noticed his self-confidence is not what it used to be. There is a level of self-loathing that breaks my heart. I am his wife. I love him. I am so proud he is a part of American history. I am proud of what he has done. I wish with everything I am, he could see himself as I see him. I know he is a genuinely good man. I know he has a good heart. For the longest time, I just didn't understand why he was being so hard on himself. Why was he keeping a wall between us? I kept thinking I wanted him to change back to the person he was before the deployment. What I really craved was the connection before the deployment, which we had never regained.

At the end of last year, we ended up in a bad situation. He was in a depression so deep he felt he didn't deserve my love or anyone else's. He felt he could never live up to my expectation of someday being "back to normal." He felt I deserved better. He said and did things trying to push me away and trying to end our marriage. I misunderstood so many aspects of our new normalcy and I judged him. I attached a stigma to him he couldn't accept and he felt he had served his country to come home and lose it all. I was tired of being the buffer between PTSD and our kids, our family and friends. I was tired of making excuses and apologies for things I didn't even understand.

I was on the verge of walking away. He had hurt me, and I felt I didn't deserve it. For a few days, I tried to formulate a plan for what my life would be without him. I then realized I couldn't even imagine my life without him. My love for him was greater than the hurt and anger I was feeling. Stubbornness kicked in, I put my foot down and told him I refused to accept this. I refused to let my marriage end. I refused to lose him. No matter how hard it was to repair, our marriage was worth it. Our love story deserved for us to fight through this. I looked him in his eyes and told him I knew his actions were not reflective of the man I knew. I didn't know why he was acting this way, but I was going to figure it out, and most importantly, I was going to love him through it. I wasn't leaving.

You can say what you want about God and faith and prayer and whether or not you believe or don't believe. I'm not here to discuss religion of any kind. All I know is in my desperate hour of need, I began to pour my heart out in prayer. I prayed for my husband. I prayed for myself. I prayed above all else for understanding. I believe I gained understanding, and it has helped my husband finally begin to heal. He is comfortable sharing his feelings with me now. He knows I don't judge him, which is what he needed all along. And once again, I am feeling the connection I longed for.

While my husband was deployed, I would tell myself, "Someday this will be over." That is what got me through each day. I knew he would come home and get out of the Marines and I presumed our life would be "normal." I would daydream about not having to miss another holiday because he was gone. I dreamt about him being able to be home on my birthday and our children's birthdays. I thought once he was out, everything which came along with him being a Marine would be over. Boy was I wrong!

One night, he was browsing Facebook and came across a posting by the mother of one of the Marines who died during his deployment. He became irate. He couldn't let it go. He had to get out how he felt and it wasn't pretty. I suggested, innocently enough I thought at the time, he just "unfriend" the mother of the fallen Marine if things she said were going to upset him that much. He looked at me as if I had just punched him in the stomach. He was angry with me for even suggesting it. He said whether it made him upset or not, there was NO WAY he was going to not be there for the mother of one of his guys. He truly felt it was disrespectful to the memory of the fallen Marine to even think it, let alone speak it. I left my husband to stew on our living-room couch to make a snack for our kids. As I stood at the stove, it hit me. "It is never really over!" Yes, he is out now, and able to be here for our birthdays, anniversaries, school programs, sporting events, and even ordinary days, but he is still and will forever be a Marine. He believes in his heart being a Marine is more than saying it. It means living it. He will be a Marine until his last breath.

I stood at the stove, tears streaming down my cheeks as my heart once again swelled with pride. I felt awful for not realizing it sooner, but it was so freeing to realize this truth. I found myself saying, "I'm Okay with this!" I'm so grateful he isn't the kind of person who served our country for the wrong reasons. He joined the Marines because of his love for America, and as he accepted his Eagle Globe and Anchor, he was completely and forever changed. I am more than okay with this, I am proud of this.

I have also come to understand that my husband, along with every other Marine Corps Infantryman, has two sides. The side of him I know is the human being. I love this human being with my soul. He is an amazing human being, capable of so much love, and so much good. The other side of him is what I call The Machine. It is what he becomes when he is in a combat situation. It is what the USMC trained him to become. They did a good job.

During the deployment, he became The Machine. Marines know they are each an integral part of The Machine. They know each individual must function to the highest level or The Machine breaks and when The Machine breaks, bad things happen. They function as a well-oiled machine. They identify threats and eliminate them. They accept orders without question and carry them out to the fullest. The Machine does not have human emotions; The Machine churns on and on, day after day. The Marines are proud of The Machine they create. They know it functions at maximum capacity and eliminates anything which threatens its functionality.

Then The Machine shuts down and coughs out the human beings. The human beings go home to families who don't understand; a society which labels them. A stigma they can't escape. The human being is a good person, but the human being has a memory. The human being remembers what The Machine did during combat and feels as if the people who profess to love him knew what The Machine did, they would be horrified and they wouldn't love him anymore. The human being has feelings of guilt mixed with the pride he feels for the job he did as The Machine. The human being feels isolated. None of his family or friends really know him as his Marines do, but they are all gone. The human being is tortured every minute of every day of his life with memories of the functions of The Machine. All the human being needs is for people to understand him. What he really needs is for those who say they love him to understand he loves

91

them too, but he is different now, and it may never change. He may forever and always be dealing with these feelings. He needs acceptance anyways.

This is our life now. We live with the ripple effect of PTSD. Some days are awesome days, some days are awful days. This is our normal. We don't need to be judged or labeled or looked at differently. My husband is the same man he always was; only now he is a combat veteran as well. I couldn't be any prouder of him if I tried. He is a man of honor, and I will never stop loving him.

I am the proud wife of a United States Marine. Not just any Marine. I am the proud wife of a combat veteran.

The True Struggles of PTSD
Cpl. Jason Spencer USMC 0351

December 16, 1999 was the day my journey with the Marines began. I had a GED so enlisting was a long difficult road with many obstacles to overcome. I ended up having to leave for boot camp a lot earlier than anticipated, because when you have a GED, you are at the mercy of the Corps as far as numbers and MOS.

After boot at Parris Island, S.C, I went on boot-leave where I became engaged to an amazing woman, Lisa, who is still standing by my side to this day. She was as nervous as I was about being in the infantry but as SOI went on, I became honored and motivated about being a Marine's Marine. A grunt. At that time, no one could have foreseen the future and the terrible events which would take us all into combat. All we knew was we were training for the moment our country would need us. As we all know, that day came shortly after the tragic events of September 11, 2001.

As the years went by, myself along with the rest of the Marines in my unit (Wpns. Co. 3rd battalion 25th Marines 4th Mar. Div, Akron OH) kept telling ourselves our turn was coming. I would sit at home watching the news, waiting for the phone to ring saying we were being activated month after month. Several of my friends had already been deployed or were getting ready to deploy and it was driving me nuts. I would go online and volunteer with any unit needing more numbers because the wait was killing me. This "black cloud" was affecting my life, job, family, everything about me. I was finally able to get orders for a TAD to range control at Quantico in June 2004.

During my time at Quantico, I worked with a group of outstanding Marines. It was a big adjustment for my family but for me it felt like I was finally able to relax and focus on where my head needed to be. Being on active duty allowed me to get in great shape and to get some much needed trigger time on just about every weapon being used in the infantry. The downside was, I was out of touch with my old unit and felt sort of outcast by them for leaving and going on active duty. The black cloud still hung over our heads and was like an elephant in the room for my entire family. One day in late October, I picked up a copy of *Marine Times* and read our unit was being activated. It wasn't long after I read the article, my Company Gunny called me into his office to officially inform me of my unit being called up. What I had not expected was the option to stay on orders at range control or return to my old unit and deploy to Iraq with them. The decision was a no brainer for me; I was going with my Marines.

I signed my orders and started packing up the family to move back to Ohio. I think everyone was happy to be moving back, but at the same time we all knew why. The time came to say goodbye a month after we returned. One of the hardest things I ever had to do in my life was look at my youngest son, give him a hug and kiss, and not know if I was ever going to see him again. It was so hard because he was still a baby and had no idea what was happening; and I had no way to make him understand. My wife remained pretty strong on the outside, as did the kids; as much as they could anyway.

We reported to the drill center and began the pre-deployment paperwork: wills, power of attorneys, etc. A few days later, we loaded our gear onto planes at Cleveland Airport to 29 Palms, for our deployment workup. During that short time, all we could think about was getting some libo in Las Vegas, because we were going to see our wives and families one last time. The down side to those couple days was the black cloud being directly overhead and we knew at any moment the rain would begin to fall. Everyone tried to have fun but most of us had a strong feeling as soon as we returned to 29 Palms we would be packing for Iraq. Sure enough, that's what happened.

Most of us had a good idea where we were going to be stationed once we landed in Iraq. The bulk of our company went to Haditha Dam, while some of us, including me, were to be stationed at F.O.B Hit. Not long after arriving at Al Asad, we loaded trucks and headed to our bases. Those of us heading to FOB Hit had already been told stories about the base receiving a lot of indirect fire and suicide bombers, but had no idea how bad it was.

As we set out across the desert, we realized how in the middle of nowhere we really were. Not 30 minutes after we arrived at the FOB, a suicide car bomb blew up at the ECP. Not long after, three mortars and a couple rockets followed and we now had a clear picture this was going to be a long, hard seven months. My platoon was assigned to MSR security and was a mobile assault platoon. Throughout the deployment, we encountered mines, IED's, suicide bombers and firefights. We had hundreds of incidents of indirect fire landing inside the wire. It happened almost daily. Our company lost 48 Marines and Corpsman during our 2005 deployment. With that brief overview said, and very brief it is, I'm going to get into the continuing war. The silent war many of us still fight in our heads every day: PTSD.

When our unit returned to Camp Lejeune, some of our wives came to see us. They couldn't wait the few days for us to return to Ohio, mine included. I went out into town and got a room at a hotel we stayed in when I was in SOI. I was standing on the balcony when she pulled in to the parking lot not knowing fully what to expect when I saw her for the first time. Everyone has a picture in their heads about this special moment and more often than not, that moment never lives up to the expectations in our minds. We embraced, but at that moment, deep down we both knew something was very different.

We returned to Ohio with a Hero's welcome and went our separate ways with families and friends who came to see us at the airport. The big welcome home was short lived and soon I was faced with all the normal stresses of civilian life. Bills, kids, no job to return to, and not able to receive unemployment because they overpaid me at some point a long time ago. Not long after our return, to add to the strife, was Christmas and an infection in my tooth which ended up being a double abscess in my jaw within a day of becoming septic. I struggled through the pain until Christmas was over, because that's one thing I was looking forward to that year. So Christmas night I went to the hospital and was told to take a sleeping pill and see a dentist the following Monday. That idea did not sit well with Lisa and she said we were going to a different hospital in the morning for a second opinion.

The following day we arrived at the Cleveland Clinic where within fifteen minutes of arriving I was surrounded by doctors. Scopes went in my nose, CT scans were ordered, the works. I realized how serious things were and they told me I was going to be spending a few days in the hospital. During my time there, my wife Lisa stayed by my side because I was in a lot of pain and was still having nightmares. She knew the proper way to wake me up and made sure the nurses knew I was a combat vet who recently returned from Iraq. Most nurses were ok and very appreciative of my service, but one male nurse was afraid of me. So much, he would not enter my room. It made me feel awkward but I didn't care, I wanted to be fixed and go home to my family.

Well, obviously, I'm still here today but am now dealing with a whole new struggle in my life: PTSD. For years I refused to give into the idea I may be affected by this. It took Marines from my unit at a reunion a couple years back to help me break the ice. But one thing happened I had not and could not foresee; I felt I was now labeled… Part of the stigma surrounding everyone with it.

Late in 2012 I reached the lowest point I could ever imagine possible in my life. I was tired of people looking at me different and not understanding I am still the good person they all know and love. I realized I could not live up to the expectations my wife wanted me to achieve. I began self-medicating with alcohol and drugs to try and numb the pain and heartache I was living with. Finally, I figured since I could never be the man my wife felt she needed, I would drive her away the best way I knew how. I cheated on her.

My wife is the strongest woman I know and have ever met for that matter, but I had always known that would be a deal breaker. Upon doing so, I also managed to push away my so-called-best-friend of over 20 years. Now, here I am spiraling out of control thinking this is at least going to be better for everyone else. I am no longer going to be the burden in their lives. Nobody is going to have to make excuses or apologize for me anymore. I won't be the one everyone asks, "What's wrong with him?" No longer will I be the one telling stories I find amusing to people who haven't been where I have or seen what I have and think it's disgusting and gives them nightmares, all the while making the stigma surrounding me worse without having a clue. Here I am thinking I am around friends and family that love me and respect me and my service. Boy was I wrong. Friends started to write me off and my wife started using PTSD as a crutch to blame my every action on. This whole time I felt like screaming out, "I am still the same fucking person, why can't you all see that?"

Lucky for me, my wife is a very stubborn angel and refused to give up or leave without getting to the bottom of this chaos. I call her my angel and always have because she has saved me from a lot over the years, up to and including myself. We had many long nights, talking, crying, and reconnecting like we never did since I came home from Iraq. She has experienced many moments over the last 6-8 months causing her to say, "Wow, I get it now." It took almost losing everything to gain my life back and save our marriage. Yes, I lost some people along the way and it is due to a lack of understanding of PTSD and refusal to put in any effort on their part. Casualties of the new war my wife and I fight every day.

People wonder why combat vets seek out other combat vets to become friends with. The answer is simple: understanding and true brotherhood. I believe the only way to begin healing and move forward comes from honesty with someone who truly loves you and is willing to step into the darkness. A great deal of healing can also come from other veterans and their spouses because we are all living the same life now. We were gods once on the battlefield but are now looked at as freaks from the people we were willing to give our lives to protect. Every time I walk down the street or go out in public, I feel like people are judging me for the Marine I had to be on the battlefield. This is just a hint of my life as well as most combat veterans.

Marines never stop being Marines. We continue the honor of what we were transformed into until our last breath. Because of our honor and commitment to the Corps, we never die. Our fallen live within every one of us and we continue to support our brothers' families, dead or alive, the brotherhood lives. Being a Marine isn't just serving your country. It's a life changing event which shapes you and your actions for the rest of your days. I know it is the achievement in my life I am most proud of for many reasons and is the reason I honor it so much. Semper Fi, 'til I die. I'm sure there is so much I missed but will try to follow up as things come to light.

21 Steps

Todd Samuelson

21 steps and turn, 21 seconds and turn, 21 seconds and step
This is my task, my job, my call.

21 steps and turn, 21 seconds and turn, 21 seconds and step.
You died in the dark, name unknown, you stood for us all

21 steps and turn, 21 seconds and turn, 21 seconds and step.
You died a soldier, that's all I care. I'm here now because you
were there.

21 steps and turn, 21 seconds and turn, 21 seconds and step.
You are not forgotten, this I swear. This covenant is marked by
the badge I wear.

21 steps and turn, 21 seconds and turn, 21 seconds and step.
We are the Tomb Guard, this is our call. You will be remembered
so say we all!

Together

Todd Samuelson

It is dark, I cannot see
I fear for you, do you for me?

Alone in the dark I hear your cry
I search for you I will always try

Alone in the dark, I cannot see
I will find you, please help me

For you my Brother I will not stop
I will search the dark, just give me a sign
Let me know, I'll throw you a line

I love you my Brothers, Sisters too
Hold on to the dawn, we'll see this through

The Dixie Diner Patrol
Mike Green
(A short story from the book *Nicky, Sasquatch and Pink Panthers*
www.jmichaelgreen.com)

Marine Recon is an all-volunteer outfit and it attracted a variety of characters. Some thought they were the toughest men who ever walked, some needed to test themselves, and some just wanted to be the best. As bad as some of them were in Stateside billets, the men of Team Dixie Diner were damned good Recon Marines even if they were more motley than the normal motley crew of Marines.

Chester, our point man, was from Bar Holler, West-By-God-Virginia. Coal country. He grew up "huntin' and fishin' and trompin' through the woods." Two hundred years earlier he would have been a mountain man along with Kit Carson and Jim Bridger. He joined the Army after high school and spent a few years with 82nd Airborne. He went home and began working in the mines and was miserable. Vietnam was nearly at its peak so Chester decided he should compare the Army and Marine Corps. The man was a natural in the bush. He could read sign better than any man in the battalion. More important, though, was the sixth sense he'd developed during years of hunting. He was not a big man, but appeared larger than he was because of his stature and confidence. "Slack" or second point, was from Denver. A tall, gangly, loose-limbed sort, he displayed a lot of grace when we had time for sports. His family spent weekends in the Rockies, hunting and fishing in the summer and skiing in the winter. He had a strong baritone and sang in a high school band and always led our songfests when we had time for frivolity. He joined the Corps right out of high school and heard about Recon. He's another natural in the bush and this was his second tour in 'Nam. He had been a corporal twice and was a PFC for the third time. Booze and fighting were his undoing.

Herb, a Navajo from Arizona following in his father's footsteps, was our radio operator. His old man had been a Code Talker during WWII and had earned a Silver Star on one of the Pacific Islands. Herb was a cowboy, more comfortable on a horse than on foot, but he could move through the bush like a spirit. The jungle was alien to him, but his childhood training in the scrubland of Northern Arizona had taught him how to hide and move gently without leaving signs. He also had the leg strength to carry the 25-pound radio in addition to the other gear we all carried.

Then came The Mule. A Louisiana Cajun from the Bayou country. The rest of the team were skinny, maybe 20 to 30 pounds underweight from too much exertion and too few calories. We ate canned C-rations instead of going to the mess hall since the cooks made everything they prepared taste like a mixture of boiled cardboard and dirt; but not The Mule. When we were in the rear, he would eat at the mess hall three times a day and ate C-rats between meals. To save weight on patrol we carried one meal a day. The Mule carried a case—*a case*—of C-rats: twelve meals for a five-day patrol. This man had a physique: large biceps, big pecs, well-defined abs, even lats. We made him carry the M-60 machine gun. Our M-16s weighed about seven pounds and the bullets were .223 caliber. The M-60 was a 30-pound weapon and the bullets were .308 caliber. The difference in weight between 500 M-16 rounds and 500 M-60 rounds was a whole bunch. We calculated one time that The Mule carried about 125 pounds when we started a patrol while the rest of us carried 90 to 100 pounds.

Larry was new to Vietnam and our team, Nicky New Guy in Marine slang. He was a lumberjack from Western Oregon, a brute of a man with hands that could squeeze a rock into pebbles. Like most oversized men, he was soft-hearted and kind. He had only been with us for a few weeks and no one knew him well. The Mule was due to rotate back to the World in less than a month, and we had Larry pegged as our machine gunner. He had the muscle to carry The Pig.

Our Tail-End Charley was a bantam rooster from New York City, a Puerto Rican by heritage and birth. Angel was a little man with the heart of a lion. He was always yakking and laughing and joking and playing practical jokes, but could turn into a snarling fit of fury at the drop of a hat. The TC position was very important to the team and Angel was well suited for it. He had to watch our rear to make sure we weren't being followed and that we left no signs of our passage.

Me? I was the team leader, third man on patrol right behind Ronnie. I'm a desert rat from California. My father owned an automotive repair shop and I found I had an aptitude for mechanics. I spent two years at our local junior college and received my AA, but the war in Vietnam was heating up and I wanted my piece of it, so I enlisted. Naturally, the Corps made me a mechanic and sent me to Camp Pendleton. Duty in Southern California was good, but I joined the Marine Corps to fight, not repair motors. I volunteered for recon.

We were an eight-man team, but Glenn was doing the ritual partying on R & R.

Dixie Diner had been tasked with conducting a five-day patrol in the mountains south of Camp Rock Pile. This part of Vietnam was karst—limestone deposits eroded into deep valleys—and dense, triple-canopy jungle. The Rock Pile was a circular monolith about 1,000 meters in diameter and 1,000 meters tall. Camp Rock Pile, housing a Marine infantry company, was in the valley along Route 9 below the monolith.

We caught a convoy to The Rock in the afternoon and were assigned a bunker for the night. The following morning we walked out of the wire in the midst of a platoon during their morning sweep of their perimeter, hoping any NVA watching would assume we were part of the platoon. The platoon moved about 300 meters southwest into the tree line and turned southeast. We stepped aside and let them pass us, then stayed in ambush position for about a half-hour while we listened for anything unusual and watched the grunts' back trail.

Once we were confident that the NVA weren't following the grunts, I signaled Chester to move out. Stealth was our primary method of remaining undetected in the bush. When we spoke at all, we didn't speak above a whisper. We didn't cook because of the cooking smells; there's nothing like a can of cold beans and franks for your only meal of the day. We moved slowly, sometimes less than one hundred meters an hour. Chester would move two or three or five slow, careful steps, then listen and scan the ground, the flanks, and the trees for anything out of the ordinary. Move a few steps, look and listen.

We moved about 2,000 meters and gained about 1,500 feet in elevation the first day and found a sheltered thicket to spend the night. We were now in our Recon Zone and could begin searching in earnest for evidence that NVA had been through the area. Our briefing two days before had reported the presence of an enemy regiment somewhere in this area, and it was our job to find them.

Before noon of the third day we found a small recently-used trail and Chester soon found a spot where we could observe the trail without being seen. We watched three groups of four to ten men moving east along the trail. We decided to follow the trail a bit and see where they were headed. We never used trails because many of them were booby trapped. Plus, we could easily bump into NVA coming the other way. Instead, we moved parallel to the trail, silently moving between trees and brush and rocks.

We followed the trail about 1,000 meters and stopped when Chester heard voices. We found a decent observation post above the voices where we could see a little piece of the trail. It sounded like a base camp below us. Sounds of laughter and wood being chopped for cooking fires indicated that our presence wasn't known. We watched four more small groups moving east along the trail, all carrying AK-47 rifles over their shoulders.

It was miserably hot, what we called the 99s–99 degrees and 99 percent humidity. Sitting still in the shade helped, but sweat continued to bead on our foreheads and run down our backs and arms. Our camouflage paint itched like a case of poison ivy. Most of us draped olive drab bath towels around our necks to both cushion pack straps and allow us to wipe sweat from our faces.

It was getting late and we hatted out for a less crowded neighborhood. We climbed the ridge behind us and found a small clearing where we could shoot a couple of sights with the compass and confirm our position. We called in the coordinates of the base camp and requested an artillery fire mission for just before dark when we would be out of the area.

We moved about 1,000 meters north and found a harbor site just as the cannon-cockers fired the mission on the base camp. There were probably some irate NVA back there.

At first light we continued through our RZ, not finding any fresh sign. We were moving north and west in the direction of Camp Rock Pile, knowing the mission would end the next day. Chester signaled for us to stop and waved me forward. He had found a small trail that had recently been used by a few men. The men were moving north and were probably in an OP watching Camp Rock Pile. We knew there were NVA all around us but not where or how many.

We continued moving north and west and had traveled nearly 500 meters, placing us near the crest above Camp Rock Pile. The jungle had become quiet, which usually indicated the presence of humans although our slow movement and lack of noise seldom alarmed the local fauna. The terrain had steepened and we had to ensure each step we made was stable before we placed weight on that leg. We entered a flat area with little ground vegetation and a ten-foot high rock outcrop to the right. Chester stopped to scan the area and decided it was safe. He moved along the base of the outcrop to where the foliage began to thicken.

Once we entered the thicker brush we had to reduce our intervals to less than three to five meters to retain visual contact with the man in front of us. We had moved about twenty meters inside the foliage when Chester stopped and waved me forward. Another trail, this one not used in several weeks.

That's when all hell broke loose.

Someone fired an M-16, a full magazine on automatic. The muffled sounds of someone yelling filtered through the dense brush. We all hit the dirt and wondered whether this was to be the day we died. I whispered to Chester to back off, watch the trail, and protect our front, then began to crawl toward the noise. There was no more gunfire but the yelling continued. *No, not yelling*, I thought. *Screaming... it's someone screaming!* Every Marine on the team was doing what I was doing: crawling toward the sound of a firefight. As I neared the outcrop, the screaming grew louder. Then laughing. *Laughing?* Now I was confused.

I reached Ronnie, who had left the trail before I had. He was on his stomach, his rifle on the ground, and his head on his arms—and he was laughing! My other teammates were on their knees, and they were laughing too. The whole damned team was laughing. I struggled to my feet and moved past the foliage.

Angel was doing pirouettes around the little clearing, screaming at the top of his lungs with a wild look in his eyes and plunging his Ka-Bar, first over his right shoulder and then over his left, at a little brown mass sitting on top of his pack. The little brown mass was dodging the Ka-Bar and banging on Angel's head.

> A friggin' rock ape.
> I couldn't help it. I laughed.

I was leery about getting close to Angel the way he was flinging his knife around. I retrieved his rifle and loaded a fresh magazine although that took awhile since I was laughing so hard my hands were shaking. I stood at the edge of the clearing and waved my arms but he made three circles before he noticed me. Angel had to be exhausted after several minutes of dancing, leaping, and thrusting his knife. He weighed maybe 125 and was carrying at least 90 pounds of assorted weapons, food, and water in addition to the monkey on his back. He finally stopped dancing and screamed for me to shoot the NVA although he used a considerable amount of vulgarity to get his point across.

I had to do something before those nasty looking claws or teeth made Angel into a medivac. Since the little monkey had no intention of jumping off Angel's pack, I had to prod it several times with my rifle barrel before it shrieked and jumped back onto the rocks. The monkey was maybe three feet tall and sixty pounds. It seemed to be berating me for spoiling its fun and even threw a couple of loose rocks at me.

It was a good five minutes before Angel was calm enough to tell us what happened. Turns out the monkey had jumped on his pack as he walked past the rock outcrop and he thought it was an NVA. He'd pointed his M-16 over his head and held the trigger down until the magazine was empty. When that didn't work, he pulled his Ka-Bar and started stabbing at the monkey. The monkey was beating on Angel's head with open palms the whole time.

It was another ten minutes before everyone was calm enough to become a Recon team again. We reported our position and beat feet out of the area since any local NVA would know we were there and would be looking for us.

From that day on Angel was known as Monkey Boy.

Aaron's Light
Diana Mankin Phelps

The 26 ton AAV, occupied by Aaron P. Mankin and 17 other Marines, rolled over an IED minutes before the "birds" arrived to evacuate the wounded. There was a school on the edge of the small town in Northern Iraq, with a soccer field for them to land.

Between the burning tank and the soccer field was a plot of freshly tilled soil. To reach the "birds," the wounded would need to be carried across the uneven land.

As Aaron was lying on the gurney with four Marines rushing to get him inside and head to a field hospital, one stumbled and fell. When Aaron rolled onto the dirt, he thought it would be easier to walk, since he was not injured from the waist down.

As he stood, the four Marines grabbed him, insisting he let them carry him. They explained to Aaron that he was in shock. With a raspy whisper he remarked, as he got back on the gurney, "I'm shocked that you dropped me." They were able to get Aaron on board without any further difficulty.

Being severally injured and in the midst of chaos, Aaron used his sense of humor to calm those who were so desperately trying to help him.

Aaron felt the need to contain the situation by trying to ease the tension of those who were dealing with the loss of life and the fear of losing more.

No matter what is going on around you or with you, the way you react and handle yourself will be the guide to how others deal with the task at hand.

Aaron's light always shines through, because he chooses to let it.

The choice is yours...

Kiss...
Diana Mankin Phelps

Aaron's voice was barely a harsh whisper after the intense heat of the explosion had seared his vocal cords. The one word he whispered to me, over and over was "Kiss." I would never hesitate, knowing I almost lost the chance to ever kiss him again.

An Army General had come to BAMC to visit the burn ward and asked permission to step into Aaron's room. All visitors would give the patients the courtesy of refusing. The General entered with his son, who was also in uniform, while I was out of the room. Aaron's back was to me when I stepped back in. I stood just inside the door, listening to them speak.

When he became aware of my presence, Aaron lifted his arm for me to come to his side. He looked up as I came close and whispered "Kiss." I leaned down and did as he had asked, before being introduced to the others in the room.

The General quickly said his goodbyes and as he walked to me, I noticed tears in his eyes. He hugged me with the desperation of a father, not a General, who faced the reality of what his son may one day endure.

The impact of one kiss, one word, one touch or even one look can change the course of another life in ways you will never know.

Who have you touched today? Who will you touch today? Don't miss an opportunity that may never come your way again...

This was taken 8 weeks after Aaron was injured and just before he received the Purple Heart.

Not All Heroes Wore Uniforms
Diana Mankin Phelps

We have all heard the term PTSD, Post Traumatic Stress Disorder. Most of our Heroes are trying to deal with the aftermath of "War," which has left them as severely wounded on the inside as those who show their scars and missing limbs on the outside.

There are other Heroes who suffer from PTSD, this one I call; "PARENTAL TRAUMATIC STRESS DISORDER."

When a parent is faced with the devastation of the child they knew so well, coming home from war, is no longer a person they even recognize, it is unimaginable...

Those who are injured physically as well as emotionally require constant attention during their recovery. But an unforeseen evil enters into the mix of emotions which can't be understood. Theirs and ours is a growing battle, which we just don't know how to deal with.

There are many supportive groups. As one who has been to "War" is better equipped to help those returning from "War," so are parents, who have endured their experience, able to help the ones who are just entering their own personal battle.

Our numbers are growing and the support needs to be organized.

If you are a parent who has been through so much and found your way of coping and overcoming, please reach out to parents who are lost and not realizing they too are suffering from the effects of our "PTSD."

We are all in this together and WE WILL OVERCOME!!!

Surgery After Surgery...
Diana Mankin Phelps

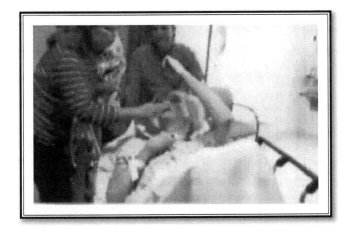

These are the wounds of war everyone can see, they are on the outside.

Aaron spent 10 weeks in combat and 10 years at war. A war of recovery that continues after more than 60 surgeries and more to come.

I can't let him go through those double doors without one more kiss. All the doctors, nurses and transport people know to stop...and give us a moment.

If only I could ease the battle that rages inside, the one only he can know. The one so many of our Heroes are fighting, that none of us can see.

We may think we have a glimpse into what a son, daughter, brother, sister, spouse or friend is struggling with...

But we do not! We never can!

Please do whatever you can to comfort, listen, cry with...just be there when that someone you know reaches out. But do not push, give them space to fight what rages inside them, and never give up.

Give back...

Caregiver
She Stays
Dustin Lenzo

My wife is my life and she is also my caregiver because of PTSD. Not only does she put up with me and the mood swings, she has to take care of our four little ones at the same time… and yet she stays.

A woman was born with a mother's intuition, but I am certain not every woman can handle being a caregiver to a PTSD riddled veteran… yet she stays.

My wife has quit a job due to my lack of patience with our children… yet she stays.

There are no words to describe how I feel about her and how grateful I am to have her. At times I feel like I am a burden because I am another child for her to care for. But she does not view it like this… and yet she stays.

I would have left a longtime ago, if I were her, because of how I treat the ones who are the most meaningful… yet she stays.

At times it seems our lives revolve around me and how I am feeling rather than anyone else and how they feel… yet she stays.

I have days where I am not close to her and the wall is built for weeks... yet she stays.

One day I was sitting here thinking, "Why is she still with me?" I thought love cannot be that strong because I have seen love be destroyed by such small things compared to what we endure... yet she stays.

I wish I could just be better, so I can be that husband she needs and wants, but I cannot be right now... yet she stays.

I want to sleep in our bed and hold her like a husband should. But something prevents me from staying in the bed at night... yet she stays.

I say do not pity me, yet I yearn for her attention like a small child and once again... she stays.

I feel like a failure to my family, but then I think something must be there because the way she looks at me and talks with me does not make sense unless something was there worth saving. But I don't see it... and yet she stays.

Some days I treat her bad and say mean things... yet she stays.

I left for nine weeks on a selfish journey to learn about PTSD and how to cope... and yet she stays.

I do not have an answer but I know she will always be here with me to walk this journey of PTSD, although the road is rough and bumpy... she stays.

Words
Daniel A. Walsh

Weapons Platoon, Fox Co 2/23, Operation Iraqi Freedom 2003

The clarity of my words,
the very composition of their essence,
fail to depict war.
Yet,
where they fail, there is meaning...
For if words were as chaotic as war
I would forever be trapped in battle
...more than I already am.

Military Life
Rebecca Marie Iriarte

Rebecca Marie Iriarte

To be a military brat is harder than it seems
Not all sparkles and laughter.

The moving
Loss of friends
Parents returning as a different person.

My father is my hero
I could never imagine the horrors he has seen
Or the pain he has endured.

A lot of people don't realize
The waiting families sacrifice too.

The pain

The feeling of loss, abandonment
Some being cut off from the world.

Military life in a
Civilian world
No one understanding the pain.

The phone calls at 2 am
The voice on the other end sounding underwater
The dropped calls after an explosion
The worry
The longing to hear the others voice
To feel their touch again
For them to return alive.

No contact for months at a time
The letters sent back and forth
Missing their children's birth
School plays
Proms
First dates
Awards ceremonies
Graduations
Birthdays
Holidays
Weddings
The little things of everyday life
Once taken for granted.

Tears of sorrowful grief when boarding busses and planes
Saying goodbye to loved ones
Not knowing if they'll come home.

Watching parents breakdown
Having to step up and take care of them
Going through the motions of everyday life
Trying to get by
To keep what sanity remains.

The world sees a strong unbroken soldier and family
But there's always another side behind all the glory.

Just trying to focus on the good things

The occasional emails
Phone calls and letters
Enjoying every moment when they come home for R&R
The tears of elated joy when they return.

This is what has made us strong and proud
I thank all Armed Forces and families for all sacrifices
I am a part of your world.

Just keep on livin' and don't give up
Focus on the good times.

I thank you for allowing me to keep my freedom of expression
We grieve for those of the fallen
You will always be remembered in our hearts
You are all heroes in my eyes

God bless
Blessed Be

The Eagle Globe and Anchor

L.K. Laskowsky

Inspired by and written for my son Lcpl B.K. Laskowsky

Photo taken by Lorilei Nash with Siren and The Machine Photography
www.facebook.com/sirenandthemachinephotography

The Eagle, Globe and Anchor
Are symbols of the Corps

The colors worn so proudly,
By Marines in peace and war

Free from wrong and pestilence,
That good men hate to see

Some men died to give us freedom
And some were blinded in the spree

Now you know the price of freedom and what these symbols mean to me.

R.I.P. Blaze
Angela Herde

Life has taught me many lessons
many I didn't want to know.
Like how to love unconditionally
and how to let it go.

Passions slowly fading
hearts must drift apart.
What I'd give to feel that fire
exploding like the start.

Your kiss stunned me with poison
like a widows dance with death.
She cried "I'll never stop loving you"
as she watched his dying breath.

Her heart keeps on mourning
a wound that never heals.
Watching a part of you die
no one should know how that feels.

Tears flow freely
a river with twists and turns.
I loved him with a passion
a fire which embers still burn.

A numb and fading soul
exists with only a breath.
I may not make it longer dear
for soon I'll join you in death.

My days just aren't the same dear
I long to feel your touch.
I thought it may be easier
if I just took a little too much.

My heart, slowly fading
as I picture your beautiful face.
Not too much longer dear
and I'll be in your embrace.

I Bite my Tongue
David Riley

I should just forget the things I've seen and done.
I sit in silence. I bite my tongue.
I'm alone in the darkness when the demons come.
Silently screaming, wishing it were done.
Praying for strength not to use my gun.
You see me as crazy for what I've seen and done.
You see me as crazy because the demons come.
You see me as crazy for who I've become.
So I sit alone in silence and bite my tongue.

The Unnoticed Hero
Rita Jiree Jackson

Photo of an acrylic painting done by Artist PJ McNalley
www.pjmcnallyvisualartist.com/

They walk among us people
Heads held high or low
All knowing of the price they paid
For freedom to be stowed

They smile, but behind those eyes
Lies pain beyond we know
We take them all for granted
We fail to give respect
For the sacrifices they've made
to give us the lives we live

Was it for honor or for glory?
We ask among our peers
Wondering and questioning
The struggles they've bared

They ask for nothing in return
Though a thank you would suffice
Months and years of agony
Behind those starry eyes

Can someone tell me why?
Don't you know the cost of freedom?
Do you even care at all?
Every battle that's been fought
Every war that's been won
Was all because of those who said
"I'll give my all for everyone!"

A Promise
Loretta Somerville

Photograph taken by Photography by Katie
www.photographybykatie09.wix.com/pbk09

As I lie in shadows of the night
Flashbacks crawl in.
Tightness in the air fills me with dread
I feel it around me, tightening.
The panic, the fear, sets in
Oh why? Oh why?
Won't they just die?
Is it pleasure from the taunting?
The pain?
I feel deep within memories
Sometimes too much to bear in my heart.
The medications sometimes dull the memories
It would be so easy to end it all,
Oh trust me.

But I made a promise to my soul
This demon, PTSD, will not win
I will stand strong and conquer in the end.
It will take time, hard work
But I promised my soul
I would win.

A Trout River

Nick Boorman

I miss my own life
Plagued by a freedom undeserved
Confused by my surroundings

Why can't life be like a trout river?
Take place between two banks
Flow at a perfect rate

I dream of taking my life,
Most days I'm awake and
When I sleep the demons push me, closer

A broke down man,
A dream in mind who's
Given up searching.

How can a fisherman be so patient?
Awaiting a fish he cannot see, yet
Have no patience for faith in which
He cannot see?

Lost in time battered, broken
Only my Secrets prevent falling.

Today I slip, unknown
When I am to fall.

By his wounds I am to be healed
By my wounds I am to die.

Eternity

Nick Boorman

Think happy thoughts, I am told
Yet demanded to fit in.
Lost in the truth told by you
For it is my fiction which keeps me glued.

I bleed thoughts you conceive as dark, unacceptable
But unseeing my past is not within my control.

A sleepless night becomes
A sleepless day becomes
A sleepless week.

Haunted of deaths by my hands
A blood shed of revenge on an innocent
Is what I am faced with.
If I sleep they come to me but
As I lie awake I hide.

Not to regret my past
It was him or me, but
The damage done is
For Eternity.

So my happy thoughts for now, subsided
With writing as my outlet I found myself divided.
Walk the walk you need of me so in publics eyes
I won't embarrass you.
So for now I drop your hand and
Alone again facing the demons,
I stand.

The End of the Darkside

Nick Boorman

Defeating evil by turning a cheek
Will never be my style I will walk
Straight into fire, pulling the ones I love
For those who have stabbed me
In the back you will lie with my enemies
To burn.

I hurt more than a man can see
I lost track of who I am to be, don't know
If I can ever again, find me.

So I build anew
Free from hate away from sin
To become who I will be.

Many of you will not accept this
Change and are listed above to lay
I've found true love in few
For you
I will die.

My trust to never come easy again
Along with my heart
I've tried to force love on people
Undeserving of my love based on
Looking acceptable to your public's eye.

Hiding my own feelings till now
I will not let these actions affect me any longer.

For this is the end of the Darkside.

Warrior
Michael Devlieger

Photograph taken by Photography by Katie
www.photographybykatie09.wix.com/pbk09

A flash-bang memory
A warrior's code
Still in the fight
A warrior's oath

Broken is my body
Strained is my mind
A warrior's will
To put the past behind

A fight for the future
Is a struggle each day
Determined to keep
My warrior's way

Drive on always
Give up never
Still in the fight
A warrior forever

Dark Heart

Michael Devlieger

Heavy is the heart that guards dark secrets
Black is the soul of the mind that keeps it
Hiding in the lights where the eyes can't see
Shadows cast sharply where only one can be
Comfortable in the skin of lies and deceit
Damned is this moment, destined to repeat
Names are forgotten, but the faces remain
Reflecting into a glistening armor of pain
No end, no escape, nowhere to flee
For no matter where I am, my company is always me
After it all I can't deny
That through it all I wonder why
It is I I fight and battle inside
My twisted emotions and diminishing pride
All wrapped up in a mind of turmoil and anger
I live each day in jeopardy and danger
Of what or who I have ultimately become
Good and bad, two halves that equal the sum
Will I survive this battle or be engulfed by the dark
That will depend on me and what's truly in my heart

Choosing
Birgit O'Rourke

I have come to the fork in the road
I do not have a map or GPS
No navigator or MapQuest

My available tools…
1. The light seeping into my heart
2. The compass of my soul

Road 1…
Shut the light out, keep walking the dim
Cold and muddy path, my head down.
Carry in my hands the bouquet of long dead roses
With the ever sharp thorns stuck in my hands.
They cause endless pain, I cannot see the pieces of
My life, they are sinking in the mud.

Road 2…
Dampness ascends, clouds part ways.
Patches of blue sky, rays of hope piercing through.
The air, crisp and sweet
Piercing hope delivering warmth.
The spark of life lifts flowers from the ground
Echoing sounds of all things natural.
The shards of my life sparkle with a radiance of faith.

The Power of my choices…..
Such an immense power in choice
With this power, I will not choose Road 1
But Road 2.

In this new year of possibilities….
I will choose to….

Remember the integrity of love TJ and I shared.
See only the core beauty of TJ's soul.
Not let TJ's or Tommy's death be in vain.
Not let their suicides define their name.
Not let their suicides define me, but rather refine me.
Let those in my life know how much I love them and need them.
Let them know how priceless and beautiful they are to me.
Cast out darkness, sorrow, self-pity and all self-destructive thoughts
infecting my broken heart.
Invite the light, joyous, free, compassionate energies of the heavens to
dance in the realms of my healing heart and soul.
Shine the healing light in to all the places dark.
Laugh as freely as I have been able to cry.
Stretch my mind and body.
Truly let my creativity flow.
Spark creativity and healing in others.
Live in the moment.
Dance, sing and invite others to dance and sing with me.
Fully feel, being clear and present in my life.

I have the power to choose…
I choose to be free.

Permanent Memorial
Brandon W. Crowell-MacClean

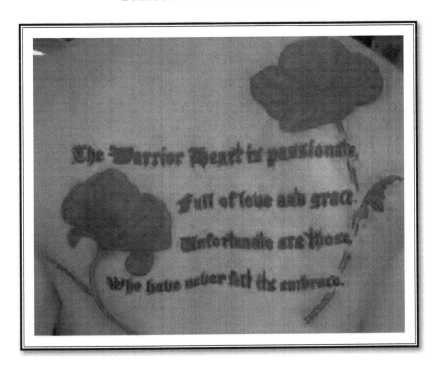

Shortly after I began going public with my writing, I was contacted by Brandon about using my poem for a tattoo. I didn't take it very seriously and told him I was absolutely good with him doing so. Several days later I was sent a photo of this man's back with a verse of my poem, "The Warrior Heart" tattooed in very large letters. I was amazed and honored. I found it hard to believe someone could feel my words so much, they would use them as a memorial for a fallen loved one. The other part of the story I was astounded by was finding out Brandon was a Canadian Soldier and the ink was a memorial for his cousin, KIA in Afghanistan. It opened my eyes to the understanding that America is not the only country fighting the War on Terror. As American Warriors, we have brothers-in-arms, domestic and foreign; and they endure the same struggles we do. I am forever humbled and honored by Brandon using my poem as the main focus to his eternal memorial. I am eagerly awaiting for the entire piece to be finished. (Artwork in picture credited to Tattoo Artist Shelby Merrithew).

-Andrew R. Jones

Andrew,

You asked me why I have chosen your words as the centerpiece to my back tattoo. Well my answer for you is: I had been searching for a design and words that need no explanation and that tell the story of the pain and suffering that the families and soldiers have gone through and still to this day have to endure. So that day when I made my mind up and said, *today is the day I find those powerful words,* I happened to come across your Facebook page via Military Minds, which I have been a member for a long time and I was reading your poems. Then I read the *Warrior's Heart* and sat there for almost 20 minutes thinking. Then I said to myself, *that's perfect*. At this time I took it upon myself to save your picture and "like" your page and contact you asking if I may use your poem for a tattoo. Not what you expected, I know, but you were more than happy about it and I am more than honored to have these words on my body for life. This piece means much more to me than a memorial; yes that's what it is, a memorial in progress far from finished for my cousin, **Pte. John Curwin 2nd battalion Royal Canadian Regiment Infantry K.I.A. Dec 13th, 2008**. One of the hardest days of my family's life. This piece also serves as a memorial for all fallen troops to show my respect for their sacrifice without greed or regard for their own life so we may live on. So please, if you know someone who has had nothing nice to say about a soldier, please give a reminder; it could be them on the front lines fighting to defend our countries. Also remind them these soldiers are fighting for change; don't let their deaths go in vain."

-Brandon W. Crowell-MacClean

A Warrior and a Horse
Andrew R. Jones

Bullets of rain impacted the barn as the occupants took cover, waiting for the ambush to pass. Mortars of thunder crashed, invoking the anxiety and vigilance within a man recently home from war. He separated from the group of loved ones and found himself on the outside of a round pen, staring at an isolated horse which, enduring her own anxiety developed from years of abuse, was known to attack.

The man decided to enter the pen, despite the eminent danger, and squared off with the beautiful creature consumed with the same unpredictable emotions as the warrior. Minutes passed as if they were hours; staring deep into each other's souls. Closing the distance cautiously… carefully… one step at a time, never losing eye contact. In this moment, a miracle occurred. The warrior and the horse lowered their brows and leaned into the other, touching ever so softly; connecting their minds, their hearts and their souls. The ambush subsided and the man exited the pen as the group of loved ones watched in astonishment.

This man is Army soldier Jason Montana. Shortly after returning home from a 22 month combat deployment to Iraq, he and his family quickly discovered he was a changed person. Arguments erupted leaving their five children in the crossfire, wondering what was wrong. Jason endured the well-known symptoms of Post Traumatic Stress: sleepless nights, quick to temper, lack of interest in activities, cold emotions and many others. After experiencing 22 months in a combat zone and motivated by Glenda Smith to share his story with me, Jason simply states, "I saw more death and dismemberment than anyone should ever have to."

In a strange twist of fate, Jason's wife and her friend were notified of two horses which needed to find a home immediately or they would be put to death. Unable to leave these noble animals to die, they bought the horses and decided to each give one to their husband. The mare, or female adult horse, had to be placed in isolation due to her aggressive unpredictable behavior. Enduring similar issues, Jason was able to see through her walls of protection and says, "I had never seen anything as this mare, she was so beautiful, but she had even more issues than I did." She was given the name Anani, Hebrew for "My Cloud," and developed a trust in the warrior which most thought would be impossible.

Jason and Anani began riding together, taking risks with their training and developing a bond only achieved between two beings which share the same pain. The healing which manifested from this relationship allowed Jason to remove his emotional barriers and connect with his wife and children once again. Acknowledging he still has a long journey ahead, he says, "I am not saying I am perfect or even back to where I was when Angela and I first met. I am saying that these gifts and our faith in the Lord are what have made me who I am today and held our family together to this day."

Taking the positivity of this miraculous experience, Jason's wife Angela has pursued training with Equine assisted psych-therapy and currently

provides services to veterans with PTSD, children with behavioral issues and a boot camp program for women transitioning from prison. This true story serves as an inspiration and a testimony of faith to all combat veterans feeling alone. Help comes in many different forms and the veteran must possess the strength to open their eyes and reach out for that help. Making the decision to start the journey of healing is not a display of weakness, rather a showcase of heroic strength.

"If you should find me wandering, just leave me be. For I'd rather be lost on my own path, than follow those who cannot see."
-Andrew R. Jones

A Passion to Inspire
Andrew R. Jones

Recruit Andrew R. Jones, MCRD San Diego 1999
Delta Company, Platoon 1085, Senior Drill Instructor SSgt Lucero
Drill Instructor SSgt Ramsey, Drill Instructor Sgt Windsor, Drill Instructor Sgt Williams

Having a passion to inspire or an inspirational passion
Is a positive way to live one's life they say.

But is it really positive when these powers
To inspire and these powers of passion are used
For what they say is evil and not for what
They say is good?

As with the most famous example Adolf Hitler
Because he was, as they say,
"One of the greatest inspirational speakers of all time,"
And to be inspirational means you must be passionate
And when a man as evil as he uses an inspirational passion
To inspire others to commit genocide…
They say it is not good…
And one should not live their life in this fashion, but that
Flows contradictory to how they say one should live with

The passion to inspire like Martin Luther King Jr. inspired
America to see colored people for who they are on the inside
And not the color of their skin and he did so using his words
Of inspiration which he delivered in a passionate way.

At the same time, another man named Malcolm X, was
Delivering his words of inspiration with his undying passion
To *force* America to treat blacks as they would whites
And he inspired passion in people to feel hate for white
Men instead of love for black men but he…
As they say…
Used his gift of passion to inspire

And if it is a gift then is it
A gift misused like the child who tears apart his
Remote control racecar in order to extract the engine
So he can connect it to a battery and make a helicopter
With the scrap pieces of the strobe light he was gifted
The previous year which will then inspire him to attend
A top ranked engineer school where he will use his passion
To design a new age of attack helicopters…
Which destroy a village…
Where a child is gifted a paper airplane
And inspired to open the folds to write a story…
Which will never be told.

"And so it is true with the gargoyles this day, for all of the angels who love them have stayed. Together they wait until days become nights, to embark on their dark and most glorious flights."
-God Bless the Gargoyles by Dav Pilkey

Amazing Andrew
Chelsea LaBarr

I had no idea what I was getting into. I knew I recognized something special in Andrew. Everyone has something special about them, but he was different. His gift did not scream out and it wasn't easily seen. He's kind, handsome and loving, but something more attracted me to him. I could feel a hidden gift that needed to be released. I knew I wanted to be around when it came pouring out.

He hid it with whiskey, amongst other things, but in the beginning, I felt guilt and sadness surrounding him at all times. Our relationship progressed and I was able to see both good and bad displayed more freely. One time, I received a phone call at 4am and answered when I realized it was him. He had been drinking and was not making smart decisions. I couldn't get off the phone until I was sure he made it home. Three hours later, the call ended and I got ready to take my Microbiology midterm. I didn't always like what I saw and often would cry by myself wondering what to do. I wanted to help but didn't know how.

I can remember the first time Andrew yelled at me. I was afraid and hurt, not because of the volume, aggressiveness, or what was said, but because I was seeing a completely different person in front of me. My heart was broken. I was confused as to how he could completely change almost everything about himself in seconds. He felt remorseful soon after the incident and apologized for what happened. I forgave him and helped come up with some appropriate responses and reactions I could use during disagreements between us in the hopes of avoiding another argument with such intensity. The next time an argument began, I responded with what I thought would be safe. I was completely wrong. Argument after argument, I was the cause of everything wrong between us. He would become so angry when he felt I disrespected him. I would cry knowing nothing I could say was going to be right, but my crying would set him off. I was completely lost and knew I couldn't be the cause of it all. It didn't take me long to realize he needed more help than I could give him.

In the beginning it was easy to let go of the negative events. As time progressed, forgiveness was replaced with resentment for all the names I had been called and how much I was yelled at and accused of trying to set him off. I was supportive, loving, loyal, and tolerant; but it never seemed good enough. Thank God for my sister and best friend Julianne. A major part of our support system, Julie was there when I needed to vent and never judged me or Andrew. My sister is amazing. When I began to distance myself, it became easier not to cry when I saw the rage.

I wanted to shake him and scream at him to get help. I didn't. Instead I would bring up counseling and how it could really help. Andrew's dad showed him an article in the paper about counseling not associated with the VA hospital that was available to him. I was excited when he told me and I would avoid the topic when I knew he was upset, but talked about it at least once a week during good times. I never told him what he should do, but would remind him of what he had told me. I waited while seeing his fridge fill with beer one night and be empty the next, hopeful he would get help soon. I saw whiskey bottles purchased at night and emptied by morning and the only thing I could do was love him and tell him I could still see a great person with a huge heart. Patience was the only thing I had to offer when I knew he drank and decided to drive around with his friend.

I listened as he talked about the guilt he felt and how angry and hurt he was while keeping an expressionless face. I tried so hard not to show him how much my heart was breaking because I couldn't make him feel better. I prayed and waited for him to choose help but prepared for the day I would get a phone call saying he was in jail or worse. Love and support was all I had to offer. I held him in my arms when he let me and thanked God for every time I could feel his heartbeat.

The final incident before deciding I was done is still too painful to talk about. I am not sure I will ever be able to forget the date or how everything human about him was gone. I have never seen a person look more soul-less while glaring at me. After he left for his class, I grabbed my stuff and left with the intention to never return. I sobbed all the way home feeling like I didn't matter. I had never loved someone so much who was able to make me feel like I was nothing. He called later and asked me to meet him. Still afraid and angry, I agreed.

I couldn't say a word. I wanted to say so much but tears flowed easier than words. Andrew said how sorry he was and he needed help. For some reason, hearing those words made me remember how to forgive him and let go of my resentment. I began to feel the anger and sadness leave me and I wanted to help him feel the same. He had already made an appointment with a counselor and promised he would try his hardest if I would still be with him. I agreed to and supported him through this journey.

Supporting him in the beginning was great. After only a few sessions of seeing Danny he seemed drastically better. Life was easier for him until the progression of his therapy halted. Arguments filled with rage reminded me Andrew was still far from being better. It was hard to encourage something I saw no further progression in, but I had faith he would continue to get better. He tried hard to push me away, but I grabbed on tighter every time. I wasn't going to give up and refused to let him give up on himself. His gift began to show more and I was committed to never leaving. Of course I didn't tell Andrew that, he would have freaked out. I was invited to a couple's session with Danny where I was allowed to speak with him one on one. I told Danny things were progressing but the rage still peaks out. I gave suggestions about what I thought would help. Soon after, Andrew was informed of *The Merritt Center Life-Transition Program for Combat Veterans* and decided to go.

Andrew came home from the first weekend with a brand new attitude. I felt peace and happiness around him where guilt and anger previously lived. He began to write more and his words were the most beautiful words in the world; I know many others share this opinion. He helps so many people by sharing his thoughts. Thank God for Danny and *The Merritt Center* for saving his life as well as the lives Andrew has helped to save.

I continue to encourage Andrew without limits. I love him more every day. He is such an amazing person and I was lucky enough to see it from the beginning. I am blessed to be able to act like a complete nerd with him every day. Some days are easier than others and we still disagree but I never question his love for me. Some people would say he was broken or lost. I'm not sure I agree. Sometimes when things seem broken they are really just unfinished, completely capable of functioning properly if someone would just attach the last part. Thank you to God for putting those missing parts where they belong.

About the Author

Andrew R. Jones is a Marine Corps Combat Veteran of the Iraq War, serving as an 0351 (Anti Tank Assaultman) with Fox Co. 2nd Bn 23rd Mar attached to 1st Mar Div RCT-1. He was a part of the initial Shock and Awe campaign in 2003 fighting from the Kuwait/Iraq border all the way to Eastern Baghdad. He also participated in Operation Noble Eagle in 2002 as well as Operation Peace Shield in Ukraine 2005. He is currently a student at Glendale Community College and plans to transfer to Arizona State University to pursue a Master's Degree in Creative Writing. He has received publications in numerous literary journals and magazines including, International War Veterans Poetry Archives and the Veteran's Writing Project core publication, The Report. He currently resides in Phoenix, AZ with his fiancée and two boys and hopes writing will lead him to finding peace while helping others along the way. Follow the progress in his mission and find more inspiration at *www.HealingtheWarriorHeart.org*.

Dear Readers and Friends,

Thank you for taking the time to read *Healing Warrior Heart*. Being able to share it with you brings great healing and purpose to all those who contributed to the book. Our life experiences teach us many valuable truths and brings wisdom which, when shared in this format, can be a treasure to all of us, and we ALL have important stories to share!

I published my book through *Triumph Press* whose mission is to be a resource for those with a passion to tell their stories and change the world by sharing their life-experience and wisdom. If you have a story you would like to share, I invite you to join the Triumph Press Community. If you explore the services and resources at **www. TriumphPress.com** and decide to publish your book, I can work with you personally, as a liaison for the publisher, to coach and assist you through the publishing process, which you in turn can do for another Triumph Author.

Triumph Press is more than a publisher; it is also a community where authors come together to find support, receive guidance, network with one other, have opportunities to share their stories in the other venues continually being developed by the community and, ultimately, feel they have a personal connection to a publisher that truly cares about their success because it is about more than the bottom line; it is about lives changed, and possibly even saved.

I hope to get to know you personally and join together
in making the world a more hopeful place!
Andrew R. Jones
USMC Combat Veteran

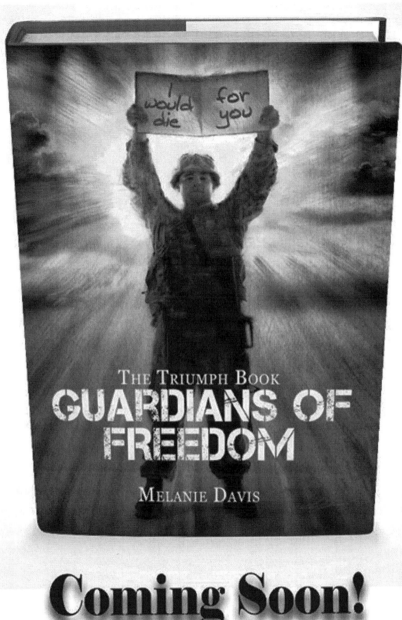

Coming Soon!

Guardians of Freedom is featuring Andrew R. Jones

Printed in Great Britain
by Amazon.co.uk, Ltd.,
Marston Gate.